WORLD LOCOMOTIVE MODELS

WORLD
LOCOMOTIVE
MODELS

George Dow

ARCO PUBLISHING COMPANY, INC.
New York

BY THE SAME AUTHOR

It can now be revealed
The first railway in Norfolk
The story of the West Highland
The first railway between Manchester & Sheffield
The first railway across the Border
The Alford & Sutton Tramway
By electric train from Liverpool Street to Shenfield
British Steam Horses
East Coast Route
The third Woodhead tunnel
Great Central (three vols)
Great Central Album
North Staffordshire Album
Railway Heraldry and other Insignia

Published by Arco Publishing Company, Inc.
219 Park Avenue South, New York, N.Y. 10003
Copyright © 1973 by George Dow
All rights reserved
Library of Congress Catalog Card Number 73–76927
ISBN 0–668–02973–0
Printed in Great Britain

INTRODUCTION

BEFORE THE STEAM LOCOMOTIVE puffed its way into the early part of the nineteenth century, to occupy the centre of the transport picture for well over 100 years, its embryonic beginnings had been manifested in the form of models. James Watt, his assistant William Murdoch, and Richard Trevithick all built working steam-models before the close of the eighteenth century. But none of them had run on rails, and the distinction of being the first to do so belongs not to a model but to a full-size locomotive, Trevithick's so-called 'tram-waggon' of 1804. Among those who followed him in the development of the steam locomotive were William Hedley (immortalised by *Puffing Billy*), Timothy Hackworth of *Royal George* fame, and George Stephenson, all of whom resorted to models for experimental purposes.

The model locomotive, then, is almost as old as the reality. And gradually, through the early-Victorian era, its potentialities came to be recognised, not only as a tool of research but as a sales-aid and, less frequently, as a recreational pursuit, usually for professionals in their spare time. Most survivals of this period, especially those made for enjoyment, are crude by modern standards, with few pretensions to scale. Several, however, are the equal of present-day models in construction, finish and scale-faithfulness to prototype, and the majority repose in museums. Some of the best of them appear in these pages.

Although this book is not concerned with the mass-produced model, it must be acknowledged that the position model-locomotive engineering enjoys today is in no small measure due to the bygone achievements of the pioneer commercial model-makers. They include the Märklin brothers of Göppingen, Georges Carette, Karl Bub and the Bing brothers of Nürnberg, Southwark Engineering Co. and Stevens' Model Dockyard of London, Clyde Model Dockyard of Glasgow, James Carson & Co. of Birmingham and last, but by no means least, the legendary Bassett-Lowke Ltd of Northampton. Their productions of model railways, locomotives, rolling-stock and castings gave an enormous impetus to modelling and, with increasing adherence to scale, eventually raised it right above the level of toys.

Another maturing influence was the growing interest of some of the bigger railway companies in the scale model for exhibition purposes, for general publicity and for staff training and education. In the latter connexion signalling instructional models were among the first to appear, soon after the turn of the century. In all these fields Bassett-Lowke excelled. In 1907–1908 three model railways, one of them of 2in. gauge and electrically operated, were made for London & North Western Railway displays at exhibitions held in Birmingham, Dublin and at White City, London. In 1910 the largest individual order ever placed for models of locomotives and

5

coaches was fulfilled by Bassett-Lowke for the Caledonian Railway. This was for no less than 30,000 clockwork-driven $\frac{1}{4}$in.-to-1ft, 1$\frac{1}{4}$in. gauge models of the 4-6-0 *Cardean* and a corresponding number of coaches; they were sold at station bookstalls for what today is the equivalent of 12$\frac{1}{2}$p (29cts) and 7$\frac{1}{2}$p (18cts) respectively. In the same year, and again in 1911, model railways were made for the combined exhibit of the Great Northern, North Eastern and North British Railways at the Brussels and Glasgow Exhibitions.

An unusual purpose for model locomotives was employed by the Crown Agents for the Colonies in 1911. A new railway was to be constructed in Nigeria, and to show the Emirs of Zaria and Katsena what the locomotives would look like, Bassett-Lowke were commissioned to make two delightful $\frac{3}{4}$in.-to-1ft scale-models of the 4-8-0 engines proposed.

Of all the pre-grouping British railway companies, the London & North Western appears to have been the biggest user of model locomotives for publicity and prestige purposes. A few were made at Crewe. Several were operable by the insertion of a coin in the slot of the plinth on which they stood. All were first-class scale-models, complete in all external detail. The author well recalls his boyhood fascination with the array of glass cases containing scale-model locomotives, coaches with fully fitted interiors, and steamships which were once to be seen at old Euston station. For many years they were grouped around the noble Great Hall, alas no more, until the London Midland & Scottish Railway swept them all away and erected in the centre a ponderous train enquiry bureau, soon to be dubbed 'the elephant house'.

But the models survived, some being repainted in the crimson lake livery of their new owner, which inherited the North Western partiality for this form of publicity. Two of them, together with others made for British Railways, similarly for exhibition purposes, are illustrated on later pages.

Other fine scale engineers eventually came on the scene to keep Bassett-Lowke company, such as Twining Models Ltd, Miller, Swan & Co. and James Beeson. Today some of them have gone too, their places taken by H. Clarkson & Son and Severn-Lamb Ltd. Their counterparts elsewhere in the world are few and far between and are chiefly to be found in Europe. The British undoubtedly preponderate amongst the best model engineers in the world. A tribute to their skill is the fact that well over half of the superb collection of scale-model locomotives displayed in the Smithsonian Institution in Washington were supplied by British makers.

In Britain several of the manufacturers, wholesalers and retailers in the business have been associated since 1944 in the Model Engineering Trade Association. It is pertinent to mention this because of the great achievement of the Association in 1951. In that year a representative of the South African Government came to Britain seeking a large range of models embracing forms of transport in the Cape and in the subsequent Union for the past 300 years. They were needed for the van Riebeeck Tercentenary Exhibition to be held in Cape Town from March 1952 onwards.

A consortium of manufacturer members of META was formed to meet this demand for craftsmanship on a grand scale and 95 per cent of the contracts were awarded to it. The total order was one of the largest ever placed for model locomotives, rolling stock, tracks and other transport equipment reproduced in 4mm. and 7mm. scales. So up-to-date was it that one or two of the 7mm. scale-model locomotives arrived in South Africa before their full-size prototypes, which were then under construction in Britain. Eventually the models enriched the collection in the Railway Museum in Johannesburg. In consequence, it has been possible to represent the locomotives of the largest 3ft. 6in. gauge system in existence.

The photographs in this book have, in fact, come largely from museums all over the world, although there are also indispensable contributions from railway administrations, manufacturers and private owners. They form a unique collection which, it is believed, is the first of its kind to be published. The order of their appearance is governed simply by the year their proto-type, or the class to which their prototype belonged, first made its appearance. By adopting this chronological basis, regardless of country, the reader is given a broad international picture of the development of steam, electric and diesel traction on railways, almost year by year, from 1804 to 1960.

There is an embarrassing wealth of material in Britain, so popular are scale-model locomotives. This is not surprising, for apart from the commercial development already mentioned, amateur builders soon became active and some coalesced into groups, the oldest of which, the Society of Model & Experimental Engineers, dates back to 1898.

Europe is also rich in material, although with some exceptions, much of it is confined to various national collections. There are fascinating arrays of model locomotives and other model-railway equipment in museums in Austria, Belgium, Finland, France, Germany, Holland, Hungary, Sweden and the USSR, some of them being the responsibility of the national railway administration. A small selection from each of these is illustrated, thanks to the co-operation of the various authorities concerned, some of whom were most generous with their assistance.

There are also known to be fine collections in Czechoslovakia, Denmark, Norway, Spain and Yugoslavia and, further afield, Egypt, but in these cases the same helpful attitude was not experienced. This, too, regrettably applied to Japan, Indonesia, Mexico and the South American countries. Here the search for material was made more difficult because of the almost total absence of museums with railway exhibits. But every South American rail-way system of importance was approached, in Spanish or Portuguese, as appropriate, and from only two was there any acknowledgement. Fortunately, the existence of a few British-made model locomotives enabled some representation to be given.

In making the final selection of illustrations, which cover scale replicas of the locomotives of 40 countries of the world, the quality of the model and of its photograph have been primary considerations. Other influencing factors have been milestones in design and development which the model represents. Models of prototypes which failed as well as those which were a resounding success are included. There is some emphasis on models of prototypes rarely seen in miniature as a relief from those which have been reproduced *ad infinitum* and, occasionally, *ad nauseam*. No distinction has been made between static and working models. And in every case the maker, owner and whereabouts of the model are indicated if known.

This book will probably appeal mostly to those who are thoroughly catholic in their admiration for fine scale-model locomotives—be they steam, electric or diesel, and for the meticulous craftsmanship put into their construction. It has been made possible only with the help of the many people and several organisations acknowledged below. To them and to all others who have supplied photographs the author records his deep appreciation.

Audlem, Cheshire   March, 1973

ACKNOWLEDGEMENTS

All museums whose model locomotives appear in this book have been indicated in the text, but the author wishes to record his thanks to certain Keepers, Curators and museum-staff who have been especially helpful. They are: British Museum of Transport, London: J. H. Scholes and R. Cogger; Järnvägsmuseum, Gävle: C. A. Alrenius; Museum & Art Gallery, Derby: Bryan Blake; Museum of Science & Engineering, Newcastle-upon-Tyne: R. Alastair and R. Smith; Museum of Transport, Glasgow: A. S. E. Browning; Ontario Science Centre, Don Mills and C. G. Slinn; Royal Scottish Museum, Edinburgh: J. D. Storer; Science Museum, London: Lt.-Col. T. M. Simmons and J. T. van Riemsdijk; Smithsonian Institution, Washington: John H. White, Junr; South African Railways Museum, Johannesburg: J. A. Caffee; Swiss Transport Museum, Lucerne: A. Waldis.

Valuable assistance has been given by officers and staff of the following railway administrations: Belgian Railways: G. Féron; British Railways: C. W. F. Cooke, John Edgington and G. H. Mapleston; Finnish State Railways: Eric Tuurna; Hungarian State Railways: Dr Alex Varga; New South Wales Government Railways: W. J. Wait; New Zealand Railways: A. N. Palmer; Southern Railway (USA): W. Graham Claytor, Junr.

Others who have materially helped with information or photographs are: Dennis Allenden, H. Barks, J. S. Beeson, D. J. Bradley, D. J. W. Brough, H. Clarkson (of H. Clarkson & Son), Richard Cole, Richard Coleby, Peter Dupen, Martin Evans (of *Model Engineer*), Jean Eynaud de Fäy, Mrs C. Finnigan (of GEC Traction Ltd), Robert Fuchs, R. H. Fuller (of Bassett-Lowke Ltd), H. Gardener (of GEC Traction Ltd), Henri Girod-Eymery, Mrs Frances de Graff, J. F. Hall-Craggs, J. Hewitson, P. M. Kalla-Bishop, G. P. Keen, Peter S. Lamb (of Severn-Lamb Ltd), Martin G. Lee, Jean Lequesne, Andrew Merrilees, Peter Olds, Humphrey Platts, James Plomer, Ross Pochin, C. R. H. Simpson, Thomas T. Taber and L. Ward.

Finally, the author is indebted to his wife, Doris, for typing and checking work; to his son, Andrew, for photography and other assistance; and to Anthony Adams for his encouragement throughout.

Britain. The beneficent power that was to change the lives and habits of mankind, the steam locomotive on rails, was the invention of a Cornishman, Richard Trevithick. Its birth-place was in Wales which today, in the twilight of steam all over the world, has by strange chance become the strong-hold of steam-operated narrow-gauge railways.

Trevithick's locomotive was described by him as a 'tram waggon'. It ran on a flanged plate-rail horse tramway, of a gauge of 4ft 2in. between the flanges, at Pen-y-darren Ironworks, near Merthyr Tydfil. Its general design was similar to that of his successful single-cylinder stationary engine, with a cast-iron return-flue boiler and steam distribution by plug-valves worked by tappet gear. Exhaust steam was turned up the chimney about three ft above the fire. The 8¼in.-diameter × 4ft 6in.-stroke cylinder was, however, located horizontally inside the boiler, instead of being in the customary vertical position. It was connected by gear-wheels to two carrying-wheels on one side of the locomotive, all four wheels revolving on fixed axles bolted to the bottom of the boiler.

These features are clearly shown in the fine ⅛th scale-model reproduced, which stands on a replica of the flanged plate-rail. It was made by W. W. Mason and presented to the Science Museum in South Kensington by Lord Wakefield of Hythe.

On 11 February 1804 the engine was tested without its wheels. Two days later it made its first historic trial trip on the tramroad. And on 21 February it demonstrated its ability to haul ten tons of iron and 70 men in five wagons the nine miles from Pen-y-darren to Abercynon at nearly five mph. More journeys were made, but its weight of only five tons proved to be too heavy for the track. So the 'tram waggon' passed into oblivion. Trevithick's second effort to arouse public interest and support, with his 1808 locomotive and circular track on the site of Torrington Square in London was likewise unsuccessful. It remained for others, above all George Stephenson, to nurse the steam locomotive into lusty childhood.

Photo: Crown Copyright, Science Museum, London

Britain. Some of the first hesitant but important steps of infancy were taken by the steam locomotive at Wylam colliery in Northumberland. It was here in 1814 that the viewer, William Hedley, supported by the owner, Christopher Blackett, and aided by Jonathan Foster, the principal engine-wright, and Timothy Hackworth, the foreman smith, produced *Puffing Billy*, among others. *Puffing Billy* was an 0-4-0, without coupling rods, but with the wheels connected by gears on one side. The two vertical cylinders were 8in. × 30in., with the ordinary Murray or box slide-valves operated through levers by tappet-rods hung from the beams and passing through ring-guides on the sides of the boiler. The latter was of malleable iron and embodied a return flue.

J. S. Youngman's ¾in. to 1ft scale-model of *Puffing Billy*, to be seen in the Museum of Science & Engineering at Newcastle-upon-Tyne, admirably recreates this venerable old locomotive in miniature. Deservedly it won the Bradbury Winter Memorial challenge cup at the 1953 *Model Engineer* Exhibition.

Photo: Museum of Science & Engineering, Newcastle-upon-Tyne

Britain. While *Puffing Billy* was being created by Hedley and his team, *Blucher* was taking shape not many miles away. This was at another Northumberland colliery, Killingworth, where George Stephenson was the engine-wright. *Blucher*

was his first locomotive, completed in 1814. It was followed by others at Killingworth and elsewhere, and in 1823 the firm of Robert Stephenson & Co. was established at Newcastle. The partners were George Stephenson, his son Robert, Edward Pease and Michael Longridge.

The first locomotive to be completed by the new firm was *Locomotion* No. 1 for the Stockton & Darlington Railway. This line was opened to the public on 27 September 1825 and was the first public railway to use steam-power. The Stockton & Darlington was the progenitor of the London & North Eastern. A splendid model of this grand old pioneer was made in ⅛th scale by T. A. Common and presented by him to the Science Museum in 1936. It portrays the prototype as it was when it ceased running in 1846.

Locomotion had two vertical cylinders 9½in. (later enlarged to 10in.) × 24in., partly recessed in the boiler. The piston-rods issued from the tops of them, and the two cross-heads, guided by half-beam parallel motions, extended over the top of the boiler to connect with four long connecting-rods, two each side of the engine. The coupled wheels were 4ft in diameter and the boiler, which had a heating-surface of some 60 sq. ft, carried a pressure of 50lb./in.² The weight of the engine in working order was nearly 8½ tons; the tender weighed 2¾ tons with its 15 cwt of coal and 240 gallons of water. Since 1892 this historic locomotive has been displayed on a pedestal at Bank Top station, Darlington.
Photo: Crown Copyright. Science Museum, London

Britain. The immortal *Rocket* was the nineteenth locomotive to be constructed by Robert Stephenson & Co. This impeccable model of it is to be seen in the Science Museum; it was made to a scale of ⅛th by Stuart Turner Ltd of Henley-on-Thames, from drawings prepared in the museum.

Rocket was a joint venture of the two Stephensons and Henry Booth, the Secretary & Treasurer of the Liverpool & Manchester Railway and originator of the screw coupling. It was completed in 1829. There is ample evidence that Robert Stephenson played the principal part in its design. And when it had triumphed at the Rainhill trials, the prize of £500 offered by the Liverpool & Manchester directors was divided between him, his father and Henry Booth.

The tubular boiler of *Rocket*, suggested by Booth, was its most important improvement. Twenty-five copper tubes of 3in.-diameter were embodied, giving a heating surface of 117¾ sq. ft, supplemented by 20 sq. ft of the copper firebox; the grate-area was 6 sq. ft. The boiler was of 3ft 4in. diameter and 6ft long. Its pressure was limited to 50lb./in.² by two safety valves, one of which was covered by a dome. A mercurial gauge alongside the chimney indicated the steam-pressure from 45 to 60lb. Two cylinders 8in. × 17in., with the slide-valves beneath them were provided at the rear end of the boiler, inclined at 35°. They drove the leading pair of 4ft 8½in. wheels, which were of oak, with cast-iron bosses and iron tyres. Total weight of the engine in working order was 4¼ tons and that of the tender 3⅛ tons.

Made partly in section, the model depicts *Rocket* as built originally for the Rainhill trials.
Photo: Crown Copyright. Science Museum, London

Eire. The first railway in Ireland was the Dublin & Kingstown (now Dun Laoghaire), which was originally built to the standard English gauge of 4ft 8½in. and was opened in 1834. It began operations with three 2-2-0 locomotives constructed by Sharp, Roberts & Co. of Manchester and, to commemorate the countries in which they were made and worked, named *Hibernia*, *Britannia* and *Manchester*.

These engines were unusual in that their two vertical cylinders, which were 11in. × 16in., were linked to the driving-wheels by means of bell cranks with 2ft 6in. arms. The leading pair of wheels were 3ft 6in. and the driving wheels 5ft in diameter. The wrought iron boiler was 7ft 6in. long and 3ft in diameter. The tender held 600 gallons of water and 1 ton of coke. Weak features in the design soon became manifest. The vertical cylinders and bell cranks produced a rocking motion enough to disturb the toughest enginemen and to damage the locomotive and track alike. So when the firebox of *Hibernia* exploded in 1842 it was not repaired. The two sister engines were disposed of in a few years. In the Museum of Transport, Glasgow, is a most realistic $\frac{1}{12}$th scale-model of *Hibernia*. The name of its maker does not appear to have survived.

Photo: Museum of Transport, Glasgow

U.S.S.R. In 1833–1834 the first Russian locomotive was built by the engineers E. A. and M. E. Tcherepanov, preceding the first public line in the country, the Tsarskoye Selo Railway, by three years. Its birthplace was a metal works in the Urals town of Nizni Tagil, where it was operated on a track of 5ft 4¾in. gauge. This pioneer was a quaint 2-2-0, completely dominated by its tall and enormous chimney. The inside cylinders were 7in. × 9in. and the boiler, 5ft 6in. long and 3ft in diameter, embodied 20 firetubes. The fuel used was charcoal. It is recorded that the engine could move a three ton load at a speed of 19 kmph.

The USSR Railways Museum displays a working scale-model of the engine, made half full-size. It was completed at the close of the last century and it stands, it will be noted, on a replica of a section of short fish-bellied rail, similar to that used by the Cromford & High Peak Railway of 1832.

Photo: USSR Railways

Britain. In 1835 R&W Hawthorn & Co. of Newcastle-upon-Tyne built their first locomotive. It was an 0-4-0 named *Comet* and was the first to go into service on the Newcastle & Carlisle Railway, the initial section of which was opened in the same year. *Comet* had 12in. × 16in. cylinders and 4ft coupled wheels. The boiler was of 3ft diameter and 7ft 6in. long and the firebox 3ft 5in. wide and 1ft 9½in. in length. The total heating-surface was 298 sq. ft and in working order the weight of the engine and tender was a little under 9 tons.

Eighty-five years later R&W Hawthorn, Leslie & Co. placed an order with Twining Models Ltd for three ¾in. to 1ft replicas of *Comet*, one of which is now exhibited in the Museum of Science & Engineering at Newcastle-upon-Tyne. They were made from old Hawthorn drawings which, fortunately, had been preserved. Each model *Comet* has a lagged boiler of polished mahogany with brass bands, the fluted sides of the brass-topped dome being finished green, as are the wheels and tender body. Indian red, a colour which became the standard locomotive livery of the railway, is used for the framing. Firebox, smokebox and chimney are black, the top of the latter, the safety-valve casing and the bands over the coupled wheels being of polished brass. Other parts, such as motion and handrails, which were iron or steel in the prototype, are finished in dull nickel-plate.
Photo: Museum of Science & Engineering, Newcastle-upon-Tyne

Belgium. Belgium's first railway was opened for public traffic in 1835. It connected Brussels with Malines and was the oldest section of the Belgian State system. Three British-built locomotives took part in the inaugural ceremony. They were No. 1 *La Flèche* and No. 3 *Stephenson*, both built by Robert Stephenson & Co., and No. 2 *L'Elephant*, constructed by Tayleur & Co., sub-contractors to Stephenson. *L'Elephant* was an 0-4-2 goods engine. In 1849 it was rebuilt at Malines workshops as a 2-4-0. Many years later SNCBM Mechanical Department pupils there made this 1/10th scale-model of the locomotive in its altered form, now to be seen in the Belgian Railways Museum.

The full-size *L'Elephant*, as rebuilt, had 5ft coupled wheels, 14in × 22in. cylinders and a working-pressure of 88lb./in.²
Photo: SNCB

U.S.A. An expanding market for locomotives encouraged many American machine-shops to turn to their production. The firm of H. R. Dunham & Co. was one that did so, but only for the brief period 1836–1839. This ½in. to 1 ft scale-model of a 4-2-0 in the Smithsonian Institution, made by Severn-Lamb Ltd, reproduces a Dunham engine built for the Harlem Railroad of New York.

The unusual location of the driving-wheels behind the firebox was claimed to increase the tractive power and stability of the engine. The driving-wheel centres were made of high-grade cast iron. The cast iron wheel later became a *sine qua non* of American locomotive design. This Dunham had 10in. × 16in. cylinders, 4ft 6in. driving-wheels and a boiler-pressure of 50lb./in.² It weighed a mere 10 tons.
Photo: Severn-Lamb Ltd

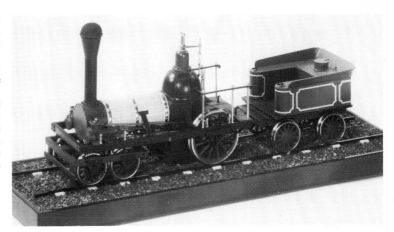

Canada. Canada's first locomotive was the *Dorchester*, the 127th to be built by Robert Stephenson & Co. of Newcastle-upon-Tyne. Nicknamed *Kitten* because of its skittish behaviour on trial runs, it hauled the inaugural train on the 5ft 6in. gauge Champlain & St Lawrence Railroad between Laprairie and St Johns, Quebec on 21 July 1836.

Dorchester weighed a little under six tons, measured 13ft 6in. in length and was carried on 4ft coupled wheels. The tender held 84 gallons of water and a cord of wood. It worked on the Champlain & St Lawrence until 1849, when it was sold to another railway and was scrapped after a boiler explosion in 1864.

This beautiful ¾in. scale replica of *Dorchester* was constructed in 1969 by Harry Allin of Bowmanville, after a great deal of painstaking research had been undertaken, and is now to be seen in the Ontario Science Centre, Don Mills, Ontario. It is built largely of brass and is operable under a few pounds of compressed air. The several-hundred rivets used had to be machined separately, for the right size was unobtainable. Many of the original cast shapes were fabricated and silver-soldered, because of the difficulty of producing very small castings. Each coupled wheel consists of 16 parts. The boiler has 42 firetubes, is mahogany-lagged and brass-bound. The model stands on a reproduction of the original track, which consisted of wooden rails surfaced by 3in.-wide iron straps spiked in place.
Photo: Ontario Science Centre, Don Mills

Britain. The 1in. to 1ft scale reproduction of the 2-2-2 *Wildfire* of the Grand Junction Railway, to be seen in the Museum of British Transport, must be one of the oldest model locomotives in the world. It was made in 1839 by John Stagg of Birmingham.

Its prototype was built in 1837 by Robert Stephenson & Co. It became No. 8 *Wildfire* in the books of the railway, but little appears to be known about its leading particulars save that it had 5ft diameter driving-wheels, 13in. × 20in. cylinders and weighed less than 10 tons. *Wildfire* played a prominent role in the inauguration of the Grand Junction Railway, the first British trunk line, which was opened between Birmingham and Warrington on 4 July 1837. It hauled the first northbound train out of Birmingham and ran nearly 12,000 miles during its initial three months at work.
Photo: Andrew Dow

Britain. Edward Bury was appointed Locomotive Superintendent of the London & Birmingham Railway in 1837, the year it was opened, remaining until 1846. His position was peculiar in that although he was a servant of the company, he was placed under contract to supply locomotives from his firm (Edward Bury & Co., later Bury, Curtis & Kennedy) and maintain them for three years at an agreed rate per mile. Because of his addiction to four-wheeled locomotives, the London & Birmingham was lumbered with 2-2-0s and 0-4-0s during almost the whole of Bury's period of office. The 2-2-0 is exemplified by the working ⅛th scale-model illustrated, made in 1840 and acquired by the Royal Scottish Museum in 1905.

The first passenger engines of the London & Birmingham possessed very similar characteristics, the single driving-wheels being 5ft 6in. and the leading wheels 4ft, set at 3ft 6in. centres. The cylinders were 12in. × 18in. and the boiler

4ft 2in. in diameter and 8ft in length, providing a heating-surface of some 387 sq. ft. Weight without the four-wheeled tender, with its primitive handbrake, was 10½ tons.

Good though their workmanship was, the Bury engines were hopelessly underpowered and it was not unusual to see four 0-4-0s at the head of a goods train.

Photo: Royal Scottish Museum, Edinburgh

Austria. Railways began in Austria in 1837 with the Rothschild-financed line rejoicing in the name of Kaiser Ferdinands Nordbahn. Its first three locomotives were built by Robert Stephenson & Co., two of them of the firm's *Planet* type. Norris of Philadelphia, however, soon came on the scene. One of the most prolific of the early locomotive-builders, Norris had turned out 232 engines by 1844, mostly for the United States and Canada. The best European customer was Austria, to which 39 had been sold.

In the Science Museum there is a well-made model of one of the last named, appropriately called *Austria*. It was built to a scale of ⅛th and is of considerable age; on its valve-chests there is inscribed the legend 'Philipp Wolf Wien 1843'.

The full-size engine went into service five years earlier, in 1838. It had 10½in. × 21in. cylinders and was carried on 3ft 10½in. driving wheels and 2ft 6in. bogie wheels. The boiler barrel was 8ft 3in. long and of 3ft 2in. diameter, with a domed Bury-type firebox; it provided some 400 sq. ft of heating surface and a grate-area of 6 sq. ft. Overall length of the engine and tender was 32 ft and in working order the weight was a bantam 14 tons. During 1839–1842 the Birmingham & Gloucester Railway (later part of the Midland) took delivery of 26 Norris locomotives, nine of which were erected in Britain.

Photo: Crown Copyright. Science Museum, London

U.S.A. The oddly named freight locomotive *Gowan & Marx* of the Philadelphia & Reading Railroad, one of the earliest of the numerous American type 4-4-0s, is represented in the Smithsonian Institution by this ½in. to 1ft scale-model.

Built in 1839 by Eastwick & Harrison, *Gowan & Marx* had 3ft 4in. coupled wheels, 12⅝in. cylinders and a working-pressure of 80lb./in.² Weight in working order was 11 tons. The design embodied an equalising lever between the two pairs of coupled wheels, devised by Joseph Harrison of Philadelphia, to achieve improved stability and riding qualities. In service *Gowan & Marx* proved to be exceptionally powerful for an engine of its size. On one run in 1840 it hauled a train of 101 loaded four-wheeled cars, totalling 423 tons, from Reading to Philadelphia at an average speed of 10 mph.

Photo: Smithsonian Institution, Washington

Holland. A broad gauge of 6ft 4⅜in. was adopted by the earliest Dutch railways, the Holland (Amsterdam-Haarlem) and the Rhenish (Amsterdam-Utrecht), which were opened in 1839 and 1843 respectively. Both began operations with 2-2-2 locomotives supplied by Sharp, Roberts & Co. of Manchester which were very similar in design.

In the Railway Museum in Utrecht there is a $\frac{1}{12}$th scale-model of No. 5 *Hercules*, one of the first Rhenish Railway engines. It was made in 1843 by J. T. F. Steenbergen of Amsterdam and is a fine example of early modelling.

Sharp Roberts had completed its prototype two years earlier. It had 14in. × 18in. cylinders, 6ft 6in. driving-wheels and a boiler-pressure of 59lb./in.²

Photo: Railway Museum, Utrecht

Britain. No information as to the origin or date of construction of this ¾in. to 1ft unpainted scale-model of a London & North Western Railway goods locomotive appears to have survived. It is to be seen in the Museum of British Transport, which acquired it in 1960.

Known as the *Crewe Goods*, the prototype is one of a numerous class constructed at Crewe works, firstly in 1844 for the Grand Junction Railway and, from 1846 until 1857, for its successor the London & North Western. It was designed by Alexander Allan, foreman of locomotives under Francis Trevithick (son of Richard), whose somewhat ponderous official title was Superintendent of the Locomotive Engine Department.

The first *Crewe Goods* engine had 13in. × 20in. cylinders, enlarged to 15¼in. × 20in. in later engines, and coupled wheels 5ft in diameter. The boilers were about 9ft 4in. in length with a diameter of 3ft 6in. The grate-area was 10½ sq. ft and in working order the weight was 19½ tons. Derivations of these Allan engines appeared in later years on the Caledonian and Highland Railways.

Photo: Andrew Dow

U.S.A. *Philadelphia* of the Philadelphia & Reading Railroad was an early American example of the 0-6-0 freight locomotive. It was constructed in 1844 by Richard Norris & Sons of Philadelphia primarily for the haulage of coal traffic, and was frequently called upon to move trains of 600 tons. The coupled wheels were 3ft 10in., the cylinders $14\frac{1}{2}$in. × 20in. and the working-pressure 100lb./in.^{2} Weight in working order was some 17 tons.

James Milholland, the master-mechanic of the company, later modified the engine, and this $\frac{1}{2}$in. to 1ft scale-model in the Smithsonian Institution shows it in its rebuilt form.
Photo: Smithsonian Institution, Washington

Sweden. Sweden's first locomotive was *Förstlingen* (the Firstling), an 0-4-0 tank built in 1847 by Munktells Mechanical Works of Eskiltuna for Frederik Sundler, contractor for the construction of the Norberg Railway. Its outside cylinders were placed between the axles, the piston-rods being lengthened in both directions, with connecting-rods driving each pair of wheels.

It was a highly unsatisfactory arrangement, and in 1853 the locomotive was rebuilt with the cylinders moved back and connected only to the leading pair of wheels, these being coupled to the trailing pair by conventional side-rods. At the same time the gauge of the locomotive was altered from three Swedish ft to the standard 4ft $8\frac{1}{2}$in. In this form *Förstlingen* had 2ft $4\frac{3}{10}$in. coupled wheels, $8\frac{3}{10}$in. × $15\frac{1}{2}$in. cylinders and weighed a mere $5\frac{3}{8}$ tons. It was put to work on the construction of the Nora-Ervalla Railway, which subsequently acquired it for ordinary traffic purposes. It was scrapped in 1856.

The model of *Förstlingen* illustrated is in the Swedish Railway Museum. It was made to $\frac{1}{10}$th scale in the Swedish State Railways workshops at Örebro and depicts the prototype in its rebuilt state.

Photo: Swedish Railway Museum, Gävle

Germany. Among the earliest locomotives constructed by Maffei of Munich for the Royal Bavarian State Railways were the class B1 mixed-traffic 2-4-0s and the class C1 goods-traffic 0-6-0s. In the Verkehrsmuseum at Nürnberg they are represented respectively by the $\frac{1}{10}$th scale-models *Donau* and *Behaim*, the prototypes of which both appeared in 1847.

The full-size *Donau* had 14in. × 24in. cylinders, 4ft 6in. coupled wheels, a heating-surface of 860 sq. ft and a grate-area of 10 sq. ft. The tractive effort was 6,170 lb. and the operational weight of engine and tender 36 tons. *Behaim* had

18in. × 24in. cylinders, 3ft 3⅜in. coupled wheels, 850 sq. ft of heating-surface and 9¾ sq. ft of grate-area. The tractive effort was 5,730lb. and engine and tender weighed 37¾ tons in working order.

Behaim was unusual, however, in that a sand-tank occupied the whole of the top of the boiler. Its object was to increase adhesion, and it was doubtless filled to capacity when the engine was used as a banker in the Fichtelbirge. *Behaim* was taken out of service in 1885 and *Donau* followed ten years later.

Photos: Verkehrsmuseum, Nürnberg

France. The locomotives of T. R. Crampton, low pitched to meet contemporary demands for a low centre of gravity, were aptly likened by C. Hamilton Ellis to a shallow-draught river-steamer on rails. They enjoyed only a limited ephemeral success in Britain, but had better luck on the Continent, so much so indeed on the Paris–Strasbourg (later Eastern), Northern and PLM Railways of France that *prendre le Crampton* became a colloquialism to go by train!

In the Science Museum there is a beautiful $\frac{3}{8}$ths scale-model of No. 122 of the Northern Railway, a Crampton built by Derosne et Cail of Paris in 1849. It is a perfect replica of the double-framed prototype, which had driving

wheels of 6ft 10⅜in. diameter in their customary position *behind* the firebox, and outside cylinders 15¾in. × 22in. The valve-chests were on top of the cylinders and inclined outwards, the valves being actuated by eccentrics through Howe's link-motion. The leading wheels were 4ft 3in. and the intermediate wheels 4ft in diameter. The centre of the boiler barrel was less than 5ft above rail-level. Its diameter was 4ft and length just under 12ft, the total heating-surface being 1,149 sq. ft and the area of the grate 15⅝sq. ft. Operational weight of the engine was 27 tons and its overall length, including the tender, 45ft.

Photo: Crown Copyright. Science Museum, London

Canada. This rather odd-looking 4-4-0 is a ¾in. to 1ft working scale-model of a locomotive of the Ottawa & Prescott which, as the Bytown & Prescott, was the first railway to enter the Canadian capital, then known as Bytown, when it was opened on Christmas Day, 1854.

It is the sixteenth built by Jack Hewitson, one of Canada's leading model-locomotive engineers, and was completed in 1968. Its boiler-pressure is 90lb./in.² and, with a length overall of 2ft 9in., it weighs 43lb. in working order. The two brass columns immediately behind the chimney and in front of the cab, which has a 'shed' roof, are safety valves, once known as steam trumpets. The model is to be seen on display at the Union station in Ottawa.

The prototype locomotive *Ottawa* was a woodburner built in 1854 with 14in. × 22in. cylinders, 4ft 6in. coupled wheels and a working-pressure of 140lb./in.² It was withdrawn about 1884, the year the Ottawa & Prescott was leased by the Canadian Pacific Railway.

Photo: James Sandilands

Austria. An unusual scale-model locomotive in the Austrian Railway Museum is *Kapellen*, which exemplifies the Engerth system of propulsion, a predecessor of the Mallet articulated locomotive, but with the front power-unit fixed instead of the trailing power-unit. Thus the wheel arrangement of *Kapellen* is 0-6-4-0 or, in Continental notation, C+B.

In 1854 Engerth, then the Austrian Government Engineer, directed the design of a special locomotive for the arduous Semmering line of the Southern Railway (Sudbahn), following upon unsuccessful trials with four engines submitted by various builders. Ten of the Engerth engines, Nos. 617–626, were supplied by Esslingen Locomotive Works, *Kapellen* being one. They had 18 7/10 in. × 24in. outside cylinders with Gooch link-motion, which actuated inclined slide-valves. The drive was to the third pair of 3ft 6½in. coupled wheels and these were geared to the leading pair of trailing four-coupled wheels of the same diameter. The working-pressure was 105lb./in.², the heating-surface 1,510 sq. ft and the grate-area 13⅗ sq. ft. In operational order the weight was 53 1/10 tons, all of which was adhesive.

In service, the Engerth engines fulfilled haulage expectations, but the geared connection was frequently fractured and, after they had run about 12,000 miles, all had it removed, making them 0-6-4 tanks. By 1860 they were either being converted to 0-8-0 tender locomotives or scrapped.

Sudbahn apprentices made the model as an 0-8-4 tank to 1/10 th scale in 1902. It was rebuilt later by the Austrian craftsman Josef Stögermayr to represent faithfully the original prototype.

Photo: Austrian Railway Museum, Vienna

U.S.A. One of the best-known locomotives in the Anglo-American world is the *General* of the onetime 5ft gauge Western & Atlantic Railroad. This is because of its involvement in a famous locomotive chase between Big Shanty (now Kennesaw) and Graysville on the Atlanta-Chattanooga line during the American Civil War. A 'double' bearing its name co-starred with Buster Keaton in a classic film which re-enacted the episode.

General was the engine pursued. It was a typical 4-4-0 of its time, having been built in the Paterson, New Jersey, shops of Rogers, Ketchum & Grosvenor in 1855. It had 15in. × 22in. cylinders, 5ft coupled wheels, a boiler-pressure of about 145lb./in.² and weighed, without its tender, a little under 22½ tons.

Texas was among the pursuers. This, too, had been constructed by a Paterson firm, Danforth, Cooke & Co. Its leading dimensions were the same as those of the *General*. Happily both escaped the scrapyard. Both were recon-ditioned and the *General*, now the well cared for property of the Louisville & Nashville Railroad, is claimed to be the world's oldest active locomotive. *Texas* has a permanent home in the basement of the Cyclorama Building in Atlanta.

The beautiful 1in. to 1ft scale-models of the two veterans are the products of the craftsmanship of Leo Myers, of Clayton, Missouri. Each took two years to build. *General* is, most appropriately, posed against a backdrop of Lacy Hotel in Big Shanty, where the kidnapping of the engine by James J. Andrews and eight Union soldiers in disguise took place on 12 April 1862. *Texas* stands on a model contemporary trestle-bridge. Since their completion these two historic model locomotives have been centres of attraction at various celebrations all over the United States. In addition, the *General*, with typical rolling-stock also made by Leo Myers, was air-freighted to Spain in 1966 for the filming of sequences in the Western movie *Custer of the West*.
Photos: Leo Myers

France. A successful and long-lived goods engine design was the outside-cylindered 0-6-0 Bourbonnais type of the Paris, Lyon & Mediterranean system, for which no less than 1,042 were built. It is represented in the Paris Musée des Techniques by this fine unpainted ⅛th scale-model made by Digeon et Fils Aîné. Part of the side-sheets at the firebox-end are cut away on each side to reveal fittings otherwise concealed.

Bourbonnais type locomotives had 18in. × 25½in. cylinders, 4ft 3½in. coupled wheels and a boiler-pressure of 143lb./in.² The grate-area was 14¾ sq. ft and the total heating-surface 1,249 sq. ft. Weight in working order was 35 tons, excluding the four-wheeled tender.

The earliest examples had a little less boiler-pressure and no dome; in place of the latter a Crampton regulator, used for many years in France, admitted steam to the cylinders. Apart from these differences, which disappeared when reboilering took place, the first Bourbonnais of 1855 could not be distinguished from the last one of 1882. PLM works at Paris and Oullins, and all the large French locomotive-builders, constructed this simple yet classic design, which was eventually to be found on other lines in France and in Italy, Austria, Russia, Spain and even Germany.
Photo: Musée des Techniques CNAM, Paris

India. One of the oldest Indian railways was the 5ft 6in. gauge Bombay, Baroda & Central India, incorporated in 1855. This ¼ scale-model 2-4-0, lent to the Science Museum by Lt. Col. J. P. Kennedy, North British Locomotive Co. and Metropolitan-Vickers Electrical Co., is a faithful replica of an English-built engine put to work when the first section of 80 miles between Surat and Baroda was opened in 1856.

Its Allan *Crewe Goods* features are instantly recognisable. The prototype engines were constructed in 1856 by E. B. Wilson & Co. of Leeds. They had inclined outside cylinders 14in. × 24in. with Howe's link-motion. The coupled wheels were 5ft and double frames were embodied in the design, the outside frames carrying the axleboxes of the leading pair of 3ft 4in. wheels. Two spring-balance lever safety-valves were characteristically provided, one being fitted to the dome over the firebox. The operational weight of the engine was some 22½ tons. The comparatively large tender had handbrakes, with the brake-blocks on the wheels on one side only.
Photo: Science Museum, London

Germany. There is a good example of a German Crampton engine in the Verkehrsmuseum at Nürnberg. It is a 1/10th scale-model of *München*, built by Maffei of Munich in 1857 for the Bavarian Eastern Railway. It had two cylinders 15½in. × 24in., 6ft driving-wheels and a working-pressure of 86lb./in.², giving a modest tractive effort of 4,450lb. The total heating-surface was 894 sq. ft and there was 12 sq. ft of grate-area. Engine and tender weighed 45 tons in working order.

Apparently it was not very successful, because in 1869 it was converted to a conventional 2-4-0. In that form it became part of the locomotive stock of the Royal Bavarian State Railways when the company was acquired in 1875, and it remained in service until 1917.
Photo: Verkehrsmuseum, Nürnberg

U.S.A. The outside-cylinder 4-4-0 locomotive is often referred to as the American type, because more than 25,000 were built in the United States, for both passenger and freight traffic, between 1840 and 1905. Some of them were extremely handsome machines, combining symmetry with elegance; some were given extraordinarily flamboyant, almost rococo, finishes. All demonstrated the basic simplicity of the steam-engine.

Phantom, a superb ½in. to 1ft scale-model of a 4-4-0 built in 1857 by William Mason for the Toledo & Illinois Railroad, and exhibited in the Smithsonian Institution, typifies all the best features of the American type.

The full-size locomotive had cylinders 15in. × 22in. and 5ft 6in. coupled wheels. The boiler-pressure was about 120lb./in.² and the weight 25 tons. The saddle supported the cylinders and secured the smokebox to the frame.

Photo: Smithsonian Institution, Washington

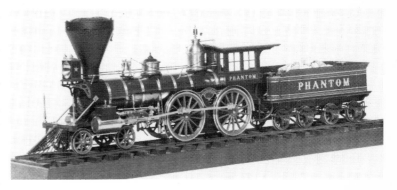

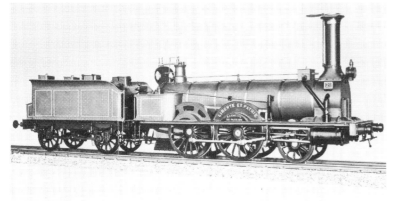

Switzerland. First section of the Swiss Western, an English ancestor company of the • Jura-Simplon Railway, was opened in 1855 between Morges, on Lake Geneva, and Yverdon, on Lake Neuchâtel. Its first Chief Engineer was an Englishman, Charles Vignoles. Nevertheless, its local predominating influence was French and nothing could be more French than its early 2-4-0 passenger locomotives, of which this model of No. 21 *Liberté et Patrie* in the Swiss Transport Museum is a faithful replica. It was made to $\frac{1}{10}$ th scale by Ing. I. Stadler and C. Schmid of Zurich in 1946–1947 to the order of the Swiss Federal Railways.

The prototype was built in the Paris works of Cail et Cie in 1858 and was typical of contemporary French design, *sans* cab and with the smokebox overhanging the leading pair of wheels. The cylinders were $15\frac{7}{10}$ in. × 24in. and the coupled wheels 5ft $6\frac{2}{8}$ in. In working order the locomotive and tender weighed 40 tons. These engines operated the Yverdon–Lausanne–Versoix (for Geneva) and Lausanne–St Maurice services at speeds up to 40 mph, or thereabouts.

Photo: Swiss Transport Museum, Lucerne

Britain. In 1859 the St Rollox Works of the Caledonian Railway produced 2-2-2 No. 76, the first of the 8ft 2in. single-wheelers of Benjamin Conner, who was Locomotive Superintendent from 1856 to 1876. No. 76 and her sisters were put to work the heaviest and fastest expresses between Glasgow, Carlisle and Edinburgh, and were the first Caledonian engines to be fitted with the Westinghouse air-brake. They were lightweight locomotives, scaling a modest 30 tons 13cwt, with outside cylinders 17in. × 24in. and a boiler heating surface of 1,169 sq. ft. The initial eight of the class were given a simple turned-over weatherboard to serve as a cab, but in later years more substantial protection for the enginemen was provided, as shown in the larger of the two photographs of a 1in. to 1ft scale-model of No. 76.

This beautiful model, complete in all external details, was completed in 1956, after some three years taken in construction by craftsmen in the workshop of the Royal Scottish Museum in Edinburgh, where it is now on public exhibition. Most of its components were fabricated or shaped from the solid to achieve accuracy and fine finish. Wheels were cut on a milling-machine and hand finished. The boiler was given properly wrapped and riveted plates, indented beneath so as to accommodate the throw of the eccentrics, as in the prototype. The smokebox is fully equipped internally and may be examined by opening the smokebox door. The near-side of the dome housing the safety-valve and the near-side cylinder, are sectional to reveal internal details. The wheels of the model are operated by an electric mechanism in the plinth, and an inclined mirror and concealed lighting give an uninterrupted reflection of the complete motion work.

opposite. Smokebox detail
Photos: Royal Scottish Museum, Edinburgh

Finland. Although Finland was thinking of railways operated by animal traction in 1849, a further 13 years were to elapse before the first line was opened. This was constructed to 5ft gauge between Helsinki and Hameenlina, 67 miles, over which the inaugural train was hauled on 31 January 1862. The locomotive was 4-4-0 *Lemminkainen*, one of four built in 1860 by Peto, Brassey & Betts at their Canada Works, Birkenhead. The others were named *Ilmarinen*, *Suomi* and *Alutar*.

Ilmarinen headed the first public train of 17 March 1862; it is illustrated by the $\frac{1}{10}$th scale-model made in 1912 by Lindell, an overseer in the Finnish State Railways workshop in Helsinki. It may be seen in the concourse of the striking station at Helsinki.

These locomotives had a character all of their own. Although their boiler-mountings proclaimed their origin, there was nothing British about the cab, the railings to the running-plate and the shape of the latter over the coupled wheels. The railings doubtless met Russian requirements, for Finland was still an autonomous, but not sovereign, Grand Duchy of the Russian Empire. The cylinders were 16in. × 20in. and the coupled wheels 5ft. The working-pressure was 120lb./in.², the total heating-surface 1,044 sq. ft and the grate-area 11 $\frac{7}{10}$ sq. ft. At 85 per cent of the working-pressure the tractive effort was 8,730lb. In operational order engine and tender weighed 48 tons. The four locomotives, and two others identical built in 1863, were designated class A1. Their maximum permissible speed was 80 kmph.
Photo: Finnish State Railways

Britain. Ross Pochin, President of the Manchester Model Railway Society, made this exquisite working scale-model of a *Coppernob*, a famous early class of four-coupled locomotive to work iron ore traffic on the Furness Railway. It is built to a scale of 4mm. to 1ft for two-rail 24-volt operation on 18mm (EM) gauge track. Its specially made motor and flywheel are located in the tender, driving the rear axle of the locomotive by means of a cardan shaft. The boiler and firebox, which is copper-plated, are formed of solid brass to secure maximum adhesion. The wheels were cut from the solid and the coupling-rods turned from silver-steel rod. The tiny builder's and number plates, the latter also carrying the company's name, were engraved. After having taken two years to construct, the model was completed in 1971, when it won two awards at the annual exhibition of the Manchester Model Railway Society.

The full-size No. 16 was one of the last *Coppernob* engines to be built for the Furness, emerging from the works of William Fairbairn & Son of Manchester in 1861. The cylinders were 15in. × 24in., the coupled wheels 4ft 6in. and the weight 36 tons.
Photo: Brian Monaghan

Britain. Although largely of wood construction, its excellent proportions and details, and especially its finish, proclaim that this miniature reproduction of 2-2-2 No. B 153 of the London, Brighton & South Coast Railway was made by an apprentice or mechanic at Brighton works soon after the full-size locomotive was completed. This was in 1862, during the *régime* of J. C. Craven as Locomotive Superintendent. Good models of the nineteenth century are rare and were seldom made by anyone but an engineer.

Built to a scale of ¾in. to 1ft, the most interesting feature is its elaborate livery, for it affords the only known example of the style of painting adopted before the advent of Craven's successor, William Stroudley. The main colour is a mid-Brunswick green, with light green and yellow outer and inner lining, some parts having additional crimson lake lining. The outside frames are claret, lined crimson lake and yellow with a black border. Splashers are also claret with black tops and borders. Boiler-bands are black with lake edges and an outer light-green lining. Chimney-cap, dome, valve-cover and handrails are of brass. The tender is similarly treated.

For many years the model was to be seen in a public house at Brighton and eventually it was acquired by Whitbread & Co. Ltd for the special decorative scheme applied to the Railway Tavern at Liverpool Street, London, in 1956. It is still there, confronting a gay phalanx of wall-plaques adorned with the heraldic devices of bygone railways.

Photo: Whitbread & Co. Ltd

Sweden. The earliest locomotives of the Swedish State Railways (SJ), the first sections of which were opened in 1856, were of British manufacture and, with two exceptions, they were constructed by Beyer Peacock & Co. A typical locomotive supplied by this firm, reproduced in $\frac{1}{10}$th scale and displayed in the Swedish Railway Museum, is illustrated. It is of class A 2-2-2 No. 33 *Widar*, and was made in the SJ workshops at Örebro in 1930.

Its prototype was the first of a batch of 20 built over the years 1863–1864, which had cylinders 15in. × 20in. and driving-wheels 6ft 1 $\frac{7}{10}$in. Steam distribution was effected by slide-valves actuated by Allan straight-link motion. The heating-surface was 941 sq. ft, the boiler-pressure 100lb./in.² and the operational weight 24⅖ tons.

The class exemplified the simple beauty of contemporary Beyer Peacock design. The livery was green with white and dark-green lining, set off by a copper chimney-top and polished brass dome, safety-valve cover, firebox band and splashers.

Photo: Swedish Railway Museum, Gävle

Britain. Models of Taff Vale locomotives are very few and far between. This $\frac{1}{8}$th scale reproduction of 2-4-0 No. 24 in the Science Museum is probably one of the best in existence. It is a working model made between 1865 and 1870 by Thomas Hopkins, then a fitter in the Cardiff (Cathays) works of the railway company, which had started building locomotives in 1856. The tender was added later.

The full size locomotive was one of a band of double-framed 2-4-0s the Taff Vale used for passenger traffic, all of them diminutive and underpowered, for the line had some stiff banks. It was completed in the Cardiff works in 1864 to the design of J. Tomlinson. The cylinders were 14in. × 20 in. and the coupled wheels 5ft. The working-pressure was only 100lb./in.², the boiler being 4ft in diameter and 10ft in length. The heating-surface was 800 sq. ft and the grate-area 11 sq. ft. Only 16 tons were available for adhesion. The weight of the engine and tender in working order was 33 tons, which included 1,000 gallons of water and 1½ tons of coal in the tender. The overall length of the two was 40$\frac{3}{5}$ ft.
Photo: Crown Copyright. Science Museum, London

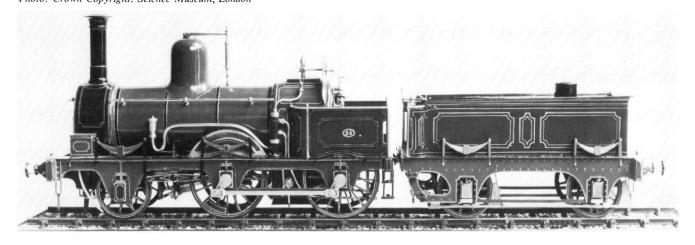

Britain. This 3in. to 1ft replica of 0-4-2 tank engine *Talyllyn* of the Talyllyn Railway was made by Severn-Lamb Ltd. Its prototype was built in 1865 by Fletcher, Jennings & Co. Ltd of Whitehaven and is still in use on the 2ft 3in. gauge line which connects Towyn with Abergynolwyn, thanks to the efforts of the first railway preservation society ever to be created. It was given a major overhaul in 1958.

Talyllyn was the company's first locomotive and was originally constructed as an 0-4-0ST, a trailing pair of carrying wheels being added in 1867. The cylinders were 8in. × 16in., the coupled wheels 2ft 4in. and the grate-area 3 sq. ft. It is believed that the original boiler-pressure was 100lb./in.² The saddle tank held 275 gallons of water and the bunkers 3 cwts of coal. Weight in working order was 8½ tons.

Photo: Severn-Lamb Ltd

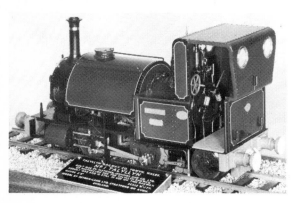

U.S.A. This rather ornate little ½in. to 1ft scale-model 2-6-0 is to be seen in the Smithsonian Institution. Locomotives of this wheel-arrangement became known as Moguls when they first appeared, because of their comparative great size and power.

The model is a replica of No. 39 of the New Jersey Railroad & Transportation Co., which was probably one of the first, if not the first, true Moguls. It was built by the Rogers Locomotive & Machinery Co. in 1865. Cylinders were 17in. × 22in. and the coupled wheels 4ft 6in. The boiler-pressure was 150lb./in.² and the weight about 36 tons.
Photo: Smithsonian Institution, Washington

Britain. There are no better-known 4-4-0 tanks than those constructed by Beyer Peacock & Co. from 1864 onwards for the Metropolitan Railway, the first underground line in the world. Several models have been made of them and one of the best is the example illustrated. It is unpainted and was built to a scale of ¾in. to 1ft by F. M. Rummens, a watchmaker who lived in Ashford, Kent and who bequeathed it to the Museum of British Transport. This beautiful model skilfully captures all the characteristics of the prototype, which in this case is No. 23 of the second batch, completed in 1866. Prominent are the large pipes either side from the cylinders to the top of the tanks; these formed the major part of the condensing apparatus for use in tunnels. Only a weather-board protected the enginemen; all-over cabs were provided in later years. The cylinders, it will be noticed, were quite steeply inclined to clear the leading four-wheeled truck. They measured 17¼in. × 24in.; with 5ft 10in. coupled wheels and a boiler-pressure of 130lb./in.² the tractive effort amounted to 12,680lb. Weight ready for service was 45 tons, the coal capacity being 1 ton and the water capacity 1,000 gallons.

Further locomotives of the class built after 1878 were slightly more powerful and had bigger coal-bunkers and tanks. They were also given Adams type sliding bogies with a central pivot, in place of the Bissel truck with which the preceding engines had been provided, the wheelbase of 4ft being unaltered. These famous engines were finished in olive green and were always well turned out, despite spending so much of their time in tunnels. The number was carried in brass figures on the front of the chimney, a Metropolitan practice for many years.
Photo: Andrew Dow

U.S.A. The world's first 2-8-0 tender engine was built at the Baldwin Locomotive Works in 1866 to the design of Alexander Mitchell, the master-mechanic of the Lehigh & Mahanoy Railroad. It was an exceptionally powerful engine for its time, having 20in. × 24in. cylinders, 4ft ½in. coupled wheels, a working-pressure of about 150lb./in.² and the greater part of its 45 tons of weight available for adhesion. The pony truck was equalised with the leading pair of coupled wheels.

It carried the No. 63 on its sandbox and was named *Consolidation* to commemorate the fusion of the Lehigh & Mahanoy and Lehigh Valley Railroads then taking place. Henceforth, the type name Consolidation was applied to future 2-8-0 locomotives, of which some 33,000 were constructed for United States railroads, making it the most numerous of all wheel-arrangements. No. 63 remained at work until 1886. Severn-Lamb Ltd made this attractive ½in. to 1ft scale-replica of the pioneer for the Smithsonian Institution.
Photo: Severn-Lamb Ltd

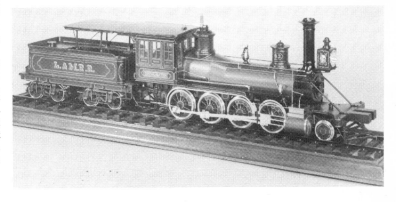

Belgium. A numerous and long-lived class of Belgian locomotive was the diminutive type 51 0-6-0 shunting tank, designed by the illustrious Alfred Belpaire. For many years Belpaire was Director of Rolling Stock in the State railway central administration in Brussels, and the characteristic 'square' firebox that bears his name was embodied in locomotives all over the world.

In the Belgian Railways Museum there is a $\frac{1}{10}$th scale-model of No. 125, made by SNCB engineering pupils at Luttre. It is a replica of one of the first type 51 engines as originally built in 1866 by the Société de Couillet. It will be seen that they had no cabs and were given stove-pipe chimneys, double smokebox doors and, most unusually, oval pannier tanks. The coupled wheels were 3ft 11½in., the cylinders 15in. × 18½in. and the working-pressure 118lb./in.² Between 1866 and 1905 no less than 470 of these engines were constructed. From 1888 onwards, cabs, rectangular pannier tanks and better-looking chimneys were provided; later still there were further changes in detail, but the basic design remained unaltered. The operational weight ranged from 26¾ tons to 33 $\frac{9}{10}$ tons.
Photo: SNCB

Britain. The Midland Railway had its headquarters and main workshops at Derby throughout its existence from 1844 to 1922. It did much for the town and its memory is perpetuated in a magnificent 1¼in. gauge, 7mm. scale fully equipped model railway, operated at 24 volts, in the Museum & Art Gallery there. This was begun in 1949 with the aid of a grant from the Carnegie United Kingdom Trustees and first brought into use two years later—one of the few to be owned by a local authority. One of its numerous locomotives is this replica of the fine old double-framed 0-6-0 No. 594, a rare example of a model of a goods engine designed by Matthew Kirtley, who was the first Locomotive Superintendent of the Midland.

Kitson & Co. built the full-size engine in 1867. It had 16½in. × 24in. cylinders, 5ft 2in. coupled wheels and a 140lb. boiler. It was rebuilt by S. W. Johnson in 1881, renumbered 2512 26 years later and withdrawn in 1928, when it was shedded at Leeds.
Photo: Brian Monaghan

U.S.A. *Sampson*, designed by J. Irving Scott and built in 1867 by H. J. Booth & Co. of San Francisco, the only locomotive-building firm on the West Coast at that time, is typical of an early American side-tank engine. It ran on the Pittsburgh Railroad of California and is perpetuated by this ½in. to 1ft scale-model in the Smithsonian Institution. The cylinders were 14in. × 18in. and the boiler-pressure 80 to 93lb./in.² The side tanks carried sufficient water and fuel for the short-distance runs on which the locomotive was employed. Its weight in working order was about 22 tons, the whole of which was available for the adhesion of its six coupled wheels of 3ft diameter.
Photo: Smithsonian Institution, Washington

Germany. With their outside frames, cylinders and high-stepping cranks there was something toy-like about the appearance of the class B6 2-4-0 engines of the Royal Bavarian State Railways. They were designed for the haulage of mail and express passenger trains.

Hans Sachs, a $\frac{1}{10}$th scale-model of which represents the class in the Nürnberg Verkehrsmuseum, was built by Maffei in 1869. Cylinders were 16in. × 24in., coupled wheels 5ft 3$\frac{3}{8}$in. and working-pressure 147lb./in.², giving a tractive effort of 5,510lb. The heating-surface was 974 sq. ft and the grate-area 14 sq. ft. In working order *Hans Sachs* and tender weighed 55$\frac{1}{2}$ tons.

Photo: Verkehrsmuseum, Nürnberg

Finland. Another early British-built passenger locomotive for the Finnish State Railways (Valtionrautatiet, or VR for short) was the class A3 4-4-0, of which Nos. 11–20 were constructed by Dübs & Co. of Glasgow in 1869. A $\frac{1}{10}$th scale-model of No. 11, made by apprentices in the VR workshops at Helsinki in the 1930s, is on display in the Railway Museum at Helsinki station.

Like the A1 engines, the cylinders were 16in. × 20in. and the boiler-pressure 120lb./in.², but the larger coupled wheels of 5ft 6in. diameter produced the lower tractive effort of 7,893lb. The total heating-surface was also smaller at 954 sq. ft, but the grate-area was a little bigger at 13$\frac{3}{10}$ sq. ft. In working order the locomotive and tender weighed slightly over 55 tons.

Photo: Finnish State Railways

U.S.A. Late in the 1860s the final link of 1,776 miles in America's first transcontinental railway was being forged. Eastwards from Sacramento, crossing the Sierra Nevada through 15 tunnels, were built the tracks of the Central Pacific, largely the work of Chinese labourers. Westwards out of Omaha were driven those of the Union Pacific, with Irishmen playing a leading part. It was planned that they would officially meet at Promontory, a shack-town in Utah Territory. This historic event took place on 10 May 1869. A woodburning 4-4-0 named *Jupiter*, of the Central Pacific, built at Schenectady Locomotive Works in 1868, confronted Union Pacific 4-4-0 No. 119, which had emerged from Rogers Locomotive Works in the same year. The last rail was laid, the last spike (a golden one for the occasion) was hammered home, and the cowcatchers of the two engines exchanged an iron kiss.

A century later H. Clarkson & Son made this exquisite pair of ¼in. to 1ft models of the two participating locomotives, which were withdrawn from traffic about 1905, neither being preserved. They are to be seen in the Smithsonian Institution at Washington.
Photo: H. Clarkson & Son

U.S.S.R. Very few details, unfortunately, appear to have survived of the prototype of this model 2-4-0 passenger locomotive in the USSR Railways Museum. It is known that it was built at the Votkinski works in 1870, for a 5ft gauge railway; that the diameters of the cylinders and coupled wheels were 1ft 3$\frac{9}{10}$in. and 5ft 6$\frac{1}{10}$in. respectively; that the boiler, which had a working-pressure of 118lb./in.², was provided with 957$\frac{9}{10}$ sq. ft of heating-surface; and that the engine was fitted with Curting's brake.

The model itself was made to ⅛th scale by P. F. and V. F. Ivanov in 1904. It is a working model, and with its brass-capped chimney, classic brass dome, slotted splashers and elaborate livery, demonstrates that Russian locomotives could be every bit as ornate as some of those of Victorian England.
Photo: USSR Railways

Canada. This is a rare, possibly unique, model of 4-4-0 wood-burning freight locomotive No. 102 of the ancient Great Western Railway of Canada. It was built to a scale of ½in. to 1ft and is in the collection of Andrew Merrilees of Toronto. A non-working model, it is finished in the original condition of the prototype, with Ramsbottom safety-valves having extremely long columns (so as to keep escaping steam clear of the driver's line of vision) and a bell mounted on the pilot beam. The tender carries a full load of cordwood, cut to scale-size in accordance with the company's specifications. The track on which it stands is a reproduction of that in use in the 1870s, flanked by correct contemporary signals.

Like its namesake in this country, the Great Western had broad-gauge track inflicted upon it in its formative years, but not Brunel's preposterous 7ft ¼in. When the expense of conversion from 5ft 6in. to standard was undertaken, a large group of 4-4-0 locomotives was ordered from Rhode

Island Locomotive Works, Providence, which built No. 102 in 1870. Some 100 engines were constructed at the time. Those destined for freight service had 4ft 6in. coupled wheels and those for passenger duties 5ft 6in. Both types had 16in. × 24in. cylinders and a working-pressure of 140lb./in.²

After the Great Western was taken over by the Grand Trunk in 1882 these engines were vastly changed in appearance by the various modifications which were made to them. A few survived to become Canadian National locomotives when the Grand Trunk was itself taken over in 1923, and the last one was scrapped in the late 1920s.
Photo: Andrew Merrilees Ltd

Eire. At the headquarters of the Institution of Mechanical Engineers in London can be seen this attractive 1½in. to 1ft scale-model of a Great Southern & Western class 21 2-4-0 locomotive. It was built in the company's works at Inchicore in 1870, the year its prototype was designed by Alexander McDonnell, Locomotive Superintendent from 1864 to 1892, and presented to the Institution by a member, John A. F. Aspinall, in 1899. The wheels of the model can be actuated by a motor in the plinth. The smokebox door opens in two semi-circular segments, the left-hand one of which is unpainted, for the whole of the offside of the model is of polished metal. The colours of the nearside are dark green, lined-out in light green and red which, together with the elegant chimney of Beyer Peacock profile and other boiler-mountings of brass, are reminders of the days before the adoption of a sombre black livery and the utilitarian and more economic cast-iron chimney.

With their tenders, which held 1,864 gallons of water and 4 tons of coal, the class 21 engines weighed only 54 tons. Cylinders were 16in. × 20in. and the coupled wheels 5ft 8½in., the tractive effort being a modest 6,720lb. In their declining years they were confined to branch line duties such as from Portarlington to Athlone and Ballybrophy to Limerick.
Photo: R. Armitage

Finland. Save only for the buffers, nothing could look more American than this beautiful model of the 4-4-0 locomotive *von Trapp* of the short-lived Hango (now Hanko)—Hyvinge (now Hyvinkää) Railway. The line was opened in 1873 and became part of the Finnish State Railways two years later. Baldwin Locomotive Works built *von Trapp* and eight similar engines in 1872. They became Nos. 63–71 of class A4 of the State system. Their cylinders were 15in. × 20in. and coupled wheels 5ft 2in. With a boiler-pressure of 120lb./in.² the tractive effort was 7,385 lb. The total heating-surface was 810 sq. ft, the grate-area 13 sq. ft and in working order the locomotive and tender weighed a little less than 47½ tons. The maximum permissible speed was 80 kmph.

The model was the craftsmanship of E. Häkkinen in the Finnish State Railways workshop at Kuopio. It was made to a scale of $\frac{1}{10}$th and is now displayed in the Railway Museum at Helsinki station.
Photo: Finnish State Railways

Britain. Few models of Edward Fletcher's locomotives appear to exist. This well finished example is to be seen in the Bowes Museum at Barnard Castle. It portrays his class 901 2-4-0 express locomotive for the North Eastern Railway, of which 55 were constructed during the period 1872–1882. It was made by R. Cairns of Darlington and was presented to the museum by H. G. T. Barningham.

The model bears the fictitious number 1882, which the maker may have used to denote the year of its completion. Its peculiar smokebox door indicates that its prototype was one of the batch of ten built in 1873 by Neilson & Co., to which Nos. 924–933 were allotted. The Neilson engines also differed from earlier members of the class by having inside frames 1¼in. (instead of 1in.) thick and a brass strip extending the length of the coupling-rod splashers. The latter is reproduced in the model. Class 901 engines had 7ft coupled wheels and 17in. × 24in. cylinders. Their heating-surface was 1,208½ sq. ft and grate-area 16 sq. ft. With their tenders they weighed 66¼ tons in working order.
Photo: Bowes Museum, Barnard Castle

New Zealand. Railways began in New Zealand in 1863 and some of the earliest locomotives were of the Fairlie articulated type. R. F. Fairlie had just patented his system, which was basically a steam-locomotive having a double-ended boiler with a firebox amidships, the whole being fixed to a frame carried by two power-bogies. The relative motion between the two was catered for by giving the reversing rod universal joints and fitting the steam-supply and exhaust-pipes with ball and telescopic joints. Thus was produced a powerful unit capable of traversing sharp curves, an asset in mountainous countries.

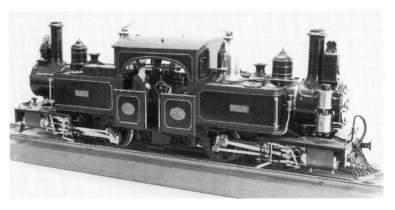

Avonside Engine Co. of Bristol built the last Fairlies of the New Zealand Railways, the six class E 0-4-4-0s of 1875. They are represented here by the $\frac{1}{2}$in. to 1ft scale-model of No. 176, made by the late Frank Roberts, once the leading locomotive modeller of New Zealand. It depicts the full-size engine about 1902, when Westinghouse air-brakes had been fitted, and is powered with an electric motor.

The class E locomotives had 10in. × 18in. cylinders, 3ft 3¾in. coupled wheels and a working-pressure of 130lb./in.² at 85 per cent of which the tractive effort was 10,200lb. The heating-surface was 847 sq. ft, the grate-area 15⅝ sq. ft and the weight in working order 37 tons. Originally allotted to the Dunedin, Helensville and Wanganui sections, they were all based on the last-named by 1886, working over stretches of 3ft 6in. track which contained 1 in 35 gradients, up which they could haul 75 tons, and five-chain radius curves. Their withdrawal began in 1899, but the last did not disappear until some 20 years later.

Photo: New Zealand Railways Publicity & Advertising Dept

Britain. The historic significance of Dugald Drummond's 4-4-0 express locomotives of 1876–1878 for the North British Railway is that the design was the archetype of many succeeding classes, not only for the North British but for the Caledonian and London & South Western (of which he became Mechanical Engineer) and, to a lesser extent, the Highland and Glasgow & South Western Railways. It is gratifying, therefore, that a fine scale-model of one of these engines is available for the locomotive student to examine and one, moreover, produced contemporaneously with the prototype. Appropriately it is to be seen in the Royal Scottish Museum, where it was made in 1883 by the staff from drawings supplied by Drummond. It was built to a scale of 2in. to 1ft, one side being in sectional form, and represents the fourth of the class, No. 479 *Abbotsford* of 1876.

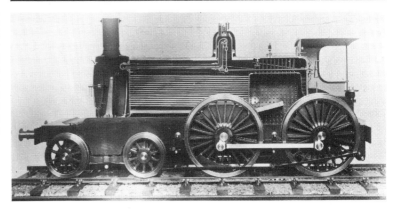

Twelve were constructed, eight by Neilson and the remainder at the North British works at Cowlairs. Their cylinders were 18in. × 26in., coupled wheels 6ft 6in. and boiler-pressure 150lb./in.² Total heating-surface was 1,193 sq. ft and grate-area 21 sq. ft. With the tender the operational weight was 75½ tons, with a little over 30 tons available for adhesion. Steam-brakes were fitted to the engine and Westinghouse to the tender. When they appeared these beautifully proportioned 4-4-0s were among the most powerful express engines in the country. And they had to be, for the undulating, sinuous Waverley main line between Edinburgh and Carlisle was their place of work almost until the advent of the present century. Rebuilt in 1902, the last of the class survived until 1924.

Photos: Royal Scottish Museum, Edinburgh

Britain. Designed by Matthew Kirtley, the 800 class 2-4-0s of the Midland Railway, of which 48 were built in 1870–1871, were celebrated in their time. Some of the drivers used to say 'they would do anything but talk.' The first to be delivered were Nos. 800–829, which were constructed by Neilson & Co. They were given 6ft 8½in. coupled wheels and 17in. × 24in. cylinders. After Samuel Johnson took over from Kirtley he was so impressed by their capabilities that between 1875 and 1882 he rebuilt the whole class, giving them new boilers with an increased heating-surface of 1,225 sq. ft and, in the case of 37 of them, 18in. × 24in. cylinders.

No. 801, which had been stationed at Kentish Town in London, was eventually transferred to Skipton shed and renumbered 36. The 5in. gauge working-model of this locomotive depicts its condition after rebuilding (in 1876) and the introduction of the famous crimson lake livery in 1883. The model was built over a period of some 1,500 hours by S. W. Baker of Ringwood. Its scale is 1 1/16 in. to 1ft and the double frames of both locomotive and tender in full-size form, together with the Kirtley valve-gear and elegant Johnson boiler-mountings, have been faithfully reproduced.

This beautiful model won a silver medal at the 1972 *Model Engineer* exhibition.
Photo: S. W. Baker

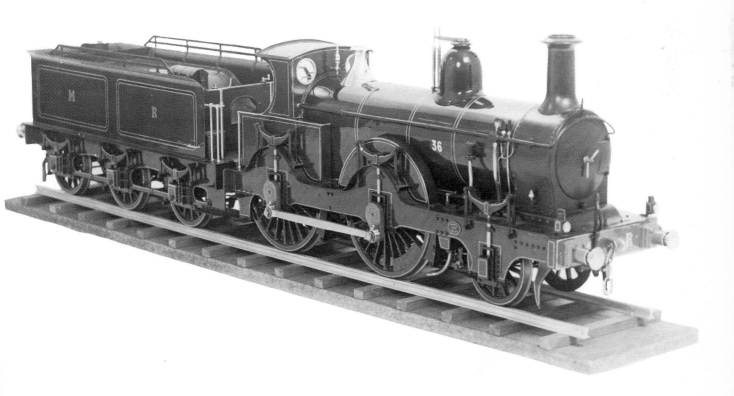

South Africa. When the Natal Government Railways took over the Natal Railway in 1875 the gauge was changed from standard to 3ft 6in. and extensions were taken in hand. The META consortium 7mm. to 1ft scale-model illustrated, which is in the Railway Museum at Johannesburg, represents one of the earliest locomotives of the new administration.

The prototype No. 6 was part of an order for seven 2-6-0 tanks, Nos. 1–7, built by Beyer Peacock & Co. and entering service in 1877–1878. Their original stove-pipe chimneys were replaced by brass-capped ones, the Salter valves on the dome were removed and the smokebox extended, all of which alterations improved their appearance. Their dimensions were modest. The cylinders were 14in. × 20in., the coupled wheels 3ft 3in. and the working-pressure 130 lb./in.² , giving a tractive effort of 9,800lb. The total heating-surface was 639½ sq. ft and the grate-area 11 sq. ft. In working order the weight was only 25 $\frac{9}{10}$ tons, including a ton of coal and 600 gallons of water.
Photo: SAR Publicity & Travel Department

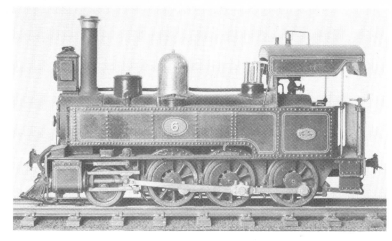

U.S.A. This ½in to 1ft Smithsonian Institution scale-model of No. 408, a mixed traffic 4-6-0 of the Philadelphia & Reading Railroad, was nicknamed *Mother Hubbard* because of its centrally located cab. Usually locomotives of this kind, which were peculiar to the United States, were called *Camel Backs*.

No. 408 was constructed in 1877 and was the first loco-motive to be given a firebox designed by John E. Wootten. The large grate-area and light draught of the Wootten firebox allowed the burning of cheap fuel, chiefly waste anthracite. Weighing 43 tons, No. 408 had 4ft 6in. coupled wheels and 18in. × 24in. cylinders. The boiler-pressure was about 120lb./in.² .
Photo: Smithsonian Institution, Washington

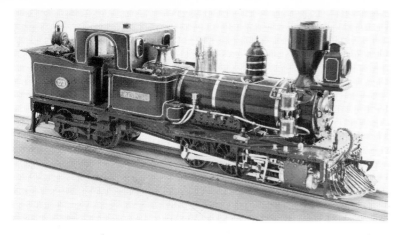

New Zealand. In 1878–1880 25 more Fairlie locomotives, again built by Avonside Engine Co., went into service on the New Zealand Railways, but this time they were of the single-boiler 0-6-4 type. The first 18 (Nos. 22, 28, 29, 32, 33, 112, 153, 187–191, 209–211 and 271–273) had 12½in. × 16in. cylinders and became class R; the remainder (Nos. 212–218) had 13in. × 16in. cylinders and were designated class S. In all other respects the whole batch was identical, with 3ft ½in. coupled wheels, 556 sq. ft of heating-surface, 11⅔ sq. ft of grate area and a working-pressure of 130lb./in.²

These engines could haul 60 tons up 1 in 35 grades and 90 tons up 1 in 50. Their normal maximum speed was 35 mph, but on one occasion a speed of 53 mph for two miles was reliably logged. No. 273 has been preserved for posterity in the shape of this fine ½in. to 1ft, 1¾in. gauge, non-powered display model. It was made by Frank Roberts and later rebuilt by W. W. Stewart.

Photo: New Zealand Railways Publicity & Advertising Dept

U.S.A. Few locomotives have had such capacious and well-lit cabs as the Forney 0-4-4 tanks of the New York Elevated Railroad. They must have been well-liked by the enginemen, because their locomotives spent as much time running in reverse as in forward gear.

Matthis N. Forney was the designer, the Smithsonian Institution ½in. to 1in. scale-model illustrated being a reproduction of No. 39 of the *El*, as it was dubbed. Cylinders were 10in. × 14in., coupled wheels 3ft 2in. and the boiler-pressure 150lb./in.² Weight in working order was only 15 tons. No. 39 was built in 1878. Similar locomotives were to be seen on the elevated lines in Chicago. By the late 1890s more than 300 of the type were in use on American elevated railways. They could negotiate curves as tight as 119ft radius.

Photo: Smithsonian Institution, Washington

Britain. In 1878 Richard Mansell, who for a brief period was Locomotive Superintendent of the South Eastern Railway, had drawings made of a proposed class of six 2-2-2 well tanks for working the Maidstone branch. They were never built, but over half a century later this immaculate model of one of them was completed and displayed at the *Model Engineer* Exhibition in London in 1930.

It is a full working-model, coal-fired, constructed to a scale of 1½in. to 1ft by G. S. and N. D. Willoughby, the gauge being 7¼in. The cylinders are 1⅝in. × 2¾in., the driving wheels 9in. and the leading and trailing wheels 6in. The copper 6in. diameter boiler embodies a round-topped fire-box 7in. long × 6⅛in. wide outside with a grate-area of 31 sq. in. There are seven brass tubes of 1in. outside diameter and 16in. long. The working-pressure is 40–45lb./in.² and the tractive effort 25lb. Engine length overall is 44¼in. and its weight in working order 1½ cwt. The attractive livery of the model is green with black bands and vermilion lining, the green wheels having a vermilion line down each spoke. Outside frames and splashers are plum red, lined vermilion, and the buffer-beams, guard-irons and leading and trailing axles are vermilion. Splendid finishing-touches are given by firebox and smokebox copings, safety-valve and dome covers and chimney-top of polished brass.

Photo: J. H. Hall-Craggs Collection

New Zealand. Locomotives of American design were first tried out on railways in New Zealand in the latter part of the 1870s. The model illustrated, made to a scale of ½in. to 1ft by Frank Roberts in about 1936, reproduces one of two 2-4-4 tanks built in 1878 by Rogers Locomotive Works of Paterson, New Jersey. They were supplied to the Rakaia & Ashburton Forks Railway, a private company in South Island. They had two 11in. × 18in. cylinders, 4ft coupled wheels and weighed 29 tons apiece. When the New Zealand Railways purchased the line in 1881 they became the first class Q engines and were given Nos. 17 and 51. They were not powerful enough to last long and both had been withdrawn by 1900.
Photo: New Zealand Railways Publicity & Advertising Dept

South Africa. Among the early locomotives of the 3ft 6in. gauge Cape Government Railways, formed in 1872, were some compact little 2-6-0s built between 1875 and 1880 by Beyer Peacock & Co., Avonside Engine Co. and Kitson & Co. They were all designated CGR 1st class, those surviving until 1910 becoming class 01 of the South African Railways. Some of the Beyer Peacock engines had inclined cylinders, as exemplified by this model in the Railway Museum, Johannesburg. It was made in 1951–1952 to a scale of 7mm. to 1ft by the META consortium.

The prototype was built in 1879. Coupled wheels were 3ft 3in. and the cylinders 12in. × 20in. With a boiler-pressure of 130lb./in.² the tractive effort was 7,200lb. The total heating-surface was 545 sq. ft and the grate-area 9½ sq. ft. The tender held 2½ tons of coal and 1,700 gallons of water. The operational weight of the locomotive and tender was a mere 37½ tons.
Photo: SAR Publicity & Travel Department

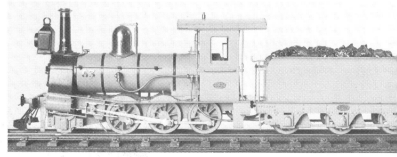

France. There was something inescapably French about the outside-cylindered 2-4-2 express locomotives which appeared on the Paris, Lyon & Mediterranean, Paris-Orleans and State systems during the latter half of the last century. The deep capuchon to the chimney, the noticeable overhang at the leading end and the high running-plate over all but the trailing pair of wheels combined to give a panache which the orderly clutter of boiler mountings did not dispel.

A beautiful 1/43.5 scale 1¼in. gauge model of PLM No. 307 made by Dennis Allenden revives all the characteristics of the famous 111–400 series of that company designed by M. Henry, the Chief Engineer. It depicts the prototype in about 1900, with original chimney and open cab, but with a four-wheeled 7½ cubic-metre tender for small branch-line work in place of the usual six-wheeled 16 cubic-metre pattern. Olive green, with very fine red lining and polished bands, forms the contemporary livery. Chimney and smokebox front are black and the buffer-beam is red with white inscriptions.

The 111–400 series were built in the PLM shops in Paris and Ouillons over the years 1879–1884, with the exception of Nos. 231–270, which Sharp, Stewart & Co. constructed. Their coupled wheels were 6ft 7in., the cylinders 19$\frac{7}{10}$in. × 24½in. and the valve-gear Allan straight-link with slide-valves. The total heating-surface, including that of the Belpaire firebox, was 1,537 sq. ft and the grate-area 24 sq. ft. The working-pressure was 147lb./in.² and the tractive effort 17,100lb. In their heyday these engines hauled the Paris-Cote d'Azur expresses and were to be seen on general passenger duties all over the PLM.
Photo: Dennis Allenden

Britain. Another Furness Railway prototype modelled by Ross Pochin is the 2-2-2 well tank No. 37, built in 1866 by Sharp, Stewart & Co. for passenger-train operation. Cylinders were 15in. × 18in., the driving-wheels 5ft 6in., the working pressure 120lb./in.² and the weight in working order was 30 tons.

As in the case of No. 16, illustrated on page 26, the scale is 4mm. to 1ft for two-rail 24-volt operation on 18mm.

(EM) gauge track. The wheels were cut from the solid and the specially made motor is installed inside the shell of the boiler, whence it is connected to a flywheel in the bunker by means of a cardan shaft.

No. 37 is constructed of brass and nickel-silver to Sharp, Stewart's original working general-arrangement drawing and was completed in 1969 after some two years work.
Photo: Brian Monaghan

PLATE I

Britain. This beautiful model of London & South Western Railway 2-4-0 No. 98 *Plutus*, resplendent in the correct contemporary livery, is preserved in the Worthing Museum & Art Gallery. It was made by W. G. Thurmott to a scale of $\frac{3}{8}$in. to 1ft, $1\frac{3}{4}$in. gauge, and portrays a type of locomotive which has rarely attracted the attention of modellers.

The full-size *Plutus* was one of the last of Joseph Beattie's seven-footers, which handled the best Salisbury and Southampton expresses in their time. It was completed at Nine Elms in 1868 at a cost of some £2,475. Its cylinders were 17in. × 22in., coupled wheels 7ft and working-pressure 130lb./in.^{2} The boiler was 4ft 2$\frac{1}{2}$in. in diameter and 9ft 8$\frac{1}{2}$in. in length, the grate-area being 17$\frac{3}{8}$ sq. ft and the total heating surface 1,102 sq.ft.

Plutus and tender weighed 56$\frac{3}{10}$ tons in working order. When finally it was withdrawn from service in 1898 it had run 976,866 miles.

PLATE II

Belgium. This delightful, beautifully finished model is exhibited in the Belgian Railways Museum. It was made to $\frac{1}{10}$th scale by SNCB engineering pupils at the Malines workshops and depicts No. 227, one of 36 class 5 2-4-0 tank engines built in 1880–1881. They were designed by Belpaire for local passenger-train services over easily graded lines of the Belgian State Railways.

The full size No. 227 was constructed by the Société St Leonard of Liège in 1880. Coupled wheels were 4ft 9in., cylinders $13\frac{3}{4}$in. $\times$ $17\frac{9}{10}$in. and boiler-pressure 118lb./in.² Operational weight was a little more than 31 tons.
Photo: SNCB

Austria. In Budapest the Museum of Communication contains a magnificent railway section which displays, amongst other things, 49 models of steam locomotives, mostly of $\frac{1}{8}$th scale, and ten of electric and diesel locomotives all made to $\frac{1}{10}$th scale. Eight-coupled goods traffic tank No. 1302 illustrated is a typical example of the high degree of craftsmanship to be seen there. It was made in the repair shops of Temesvár in 1896 to a scale of $\frac{1}{8}$th and portrays a class V.d locomotive built in 1881 for the Austrian State Railways.

The full-size engines had $17\frac{7}{10}$in. $\times$ $23\frac{3}{5}$in. cylinders, 3ft 8in. coupled wheels and a tractive effort of 12,900lb. The total heating-surface was 1,363 sq. ft and the grate-area 18 sq. ft. Weight in working order was 50 tons, including 1,580 gallons of water and 3 tons of coal. Locomotives of this type eventually became class T.IV and, later, series 450 of the Hungarian State Railways.
Photo: Museum of Communication, Budapest

U.S.S.R. Kolomna and Maltsevsk works began turning out 0-8-0 freight locomotives for Russian railways in 1878. The earliest were two-cylinder simple engines with 3ft $11\frac{1}{5}$in. coupled wheels, $19\frac{7}{10}$in. $\times$ $24\frac{3}{5}$in. cylinders and Allan's link motion. Their working-pressure was 128lb./in.² and heating-surface 1,895$\frac{3}{4}$ sq. ft. With a weight of 48 tons they were designed for operation at a speed of 45 kmph. Some later engines were built as compounds, but with comparatively few detail changes the construction of these 0-8-0s continued until 1892.

The model in the USSR Railways Museum is a $\frac{1}{10}$th scale replica of No. B 178, built at Kolomna in 1881 (works No. 625). It will be seen that it is partly sectionalised, some of the cylinder, smokebox and firebox being cut away to show internal layout and fittings.
Photo: USSR Railways Museum

Switzerland. When the Gotthard Railway was opened in 1882, some 0-6-0 tender locomotives, with outside cylinders 18 9/10 in. × 24 2/3 in., coupled wheels 4ft 4 2/5 in. and rated at 600hp, were introduced to haul express and stopping passenger trains on the Lucerne–Chiasso service. Freight trains were also dealt with on the least arduous parts of the line. They were built at Esslingen Works in 1881–1882 and were designated class D3/3. With their 4-wheel tenders they weighed 70 tons in working order, of which 44 tons were available for adhesion, and could attain a maximum speed of 55 kmph

In the Swiss Transport Museum there is a 1/10 th scale-model of No. 51. It was made in 1946–1947 by S. Hoffman of Zurich to the order of the Swiss Federal Railways.

Photo: Swiss Transport Museum, Lucerne

France. For many years from 1855 onwards the Paris–Versailles and Paris–St Germain-en-Laye suburban lines of the Western Railway (Chemin de Fer de l'Ouest) were operated by quaint little 2-4-0 tanks with tall chimneys, huge domes and a very short wheelbase; Parisians aptly called them *les bicyclettes*. They had good acceleration and a useful turn of speed when lightly loaded. A batch of 20, Nos. 101–120, was built in 1882 by Société des Batignolles. Their cylinders were 16½ in. × 22in., coupled wheels 5ft 4in. and working-pressure 132lb./in.² Tractive effort was 11,700lb. and weight in working order 38 tons.

The 1/43.5 scale 1¼in. gauge working model illustrated is of No. 103, in 1890 condition, made by Dennis Allenden. Unusual features are the coal bunker across the firebox-top and the rear door to the cab giving access to the train. The finish is mid-green, lined yellow, with polished name and number plates.

Photo: Dennis Allenden

Britain. Dr J. B. Winter's 1in. to 1ft replica of London, Brighton & South Coast class D2 0-4-2 *Como* is unquestionably one of the best examples of a scale-model locomotive ever constructed. So far as the *Model Engineer* is concerned, reference to back numbers will demonstrate that it has also been one of the most publicised. Its building began on Christmas Eve, 1884. The locomotive was finished in 1898, the contemporary elaborate livery being applied by the foreman of the paint-shop of the LB&SC works at Brighton. The tender was completed on 2 March 1915, the whole job having consumed 21,000 hours of work. Although it is a working model and was probably tested with compressed air, it is doubtful whether it would run under its own steam, for the boiler is an exact reproduction of the full size one and contains 262 tubes of only ⅛in. outside diameter. The firebox has the same number of stays and rivets as the prototype. Owing to the smallness of the pipework there would probably arise problems of condensation should steam operation be attempted. Dr Winter presented his beautiful model to Brighton Museum & Art Gallery in 1916.

The class D2 engines were designed by William Stroudley, who was LB&SC Locomotive Superintendent from 1870 to 1889. They were intended for working fast fruit-traffic between Worthing and London, and perishable merchandise from the Continent via Newhaven, but they also found a place at the head of main-line stopping and excursion trains. *Como* was built at Brighton works in 1883. The cylinders were 17in. × 24in., the coupled wheels 5ft 6in, and the total heating-surface 1,074 sq. ft. The boiler, which was 4ft 3in. in diameter and 10ft 2in. long, had a working-pressure of 150lb./in.² and at 85 per cent of that pressure the tractive effort was 15,186lb. The tender held 2,250 gallons of water and 4 tons of coal and, in working order, engine and tender weighed 63 tons 14 cwt.

Como was withdrawn from traffic in 1904.

Photo: Brighton Museum & Art Gallery

France. Fortunately for the French, only one Webb compound ever operated in France. This was the experimental 2-2-2-0 No. 901 of the Western Railway (Chemin de Fer de l'Ouest). It was built to plans of F. W. Webb by Sharp Stewart & Co. in 1884 and, apart from a French touch here and there, it was identical with the London & North Western locomotive No. 300 *Compound*, after which it was named. The drive was divided, with the inside low-pressure cylinder (26in. × 24in.) actuating the leading axle and the two outside high-pressure cylinders (13in. × 24in.) driving the trailing axle. The driving-axles were not coupled, the wheels being 6ft 7in. in diameter. The valve-gear was Joy radial, with return-crank virtual-pivot compensation and slide-valves. The working-pressure was 154lb./in.² and the tractive effort 13,800lb. Operational weight was 31 tons.

No doubt politeness restrained the French from saying what they really thought about it, for after a very short time they altered the engine by providing a longer smokebox, a chimney equal in ugliness to the Crewe product, deeper valances, different sanding-gear and the new No. 500; the name was discreetly dropped. But the engine obstinately remained unsuccessful, was ultimately abandoned and scrapped soon after 1909. This forgotten episode in compounding is recalled by Dennis Allenden's 1/43.5 scale-model, 1¼in. gauge, of No. 500 in its definitive state, with Ouest standard four-wheeled tender. The livery is mid-green, lined yellow and bordered black. The smokebox, chimney, wheels and chassis are black, the boiler-bands, plates and beadings being polished brass.
Photo: Dennis Allenden

Eire. Once upon a time there was a very odd railway in the far west of Ireland called the Listowel & Ballybunion, which was opened with some ceremony on Leap Year Day 1888. It was odd because its locomotives and rolling-stock ran on A-shaped trestled permanent way. Lartigue, its inventor, described it as a monorail. But in fact it was a kind of 3-rail system, the rail at the apex being the carrier and those at each side, near the foot of the trestles, being guide rails. Thus everything that ran upon the railway was a Siamese

44

twin, yet it was claimed to be economic because road-bed and ballast costs were negligible.

Three duplex locomotives were provided by the Hunslet Engine Co. of Leeds. Each had three coupled axles, with 2ft wheels placed between the twin boilers, the centre pair of coupled wheels being actuated by two cylinders 7in. × 12 in. The tender was carried on two 2ft coupled wheels and axles, driven by two cylinders 5in. × 7in. The twin boilers which had a working-pressure of 150lb./in.², mustered 143 sq. ft of heating-surface, the combined grate-areas being 10 sq. ft. The tractive effort at 75 per cent of boiler pressure was 2,751lb. and the complete unit weighed about 10 tons in working order.

Few models have been made of this unusual locomotive. The one illustrated, which was completed in 1970 after two years under construction, forms part of an ambitious layout of the Listowel & Ballybunion which a syndicate of four, headed by Donald Boreham of Northolt, is building for the fiftieth annual exhibition of the Model Railway Club in 1975. It has been constructed to a scale of 16mm. to 1ft and is a working model with working headlamp, the motor being installed in the tender. It is completely detailed externally, including full cab fittings, and stands on track supported by plastic heat-moulded A-shaped trestles. It carries the name *Sieglinde* only because one of the syndicate is inspired by the music of Wagner. Fortunately the footplate is a cool place in this case, for the crew is made of candlegrease.

Photo: A. Stapleton-Garner, BSc

Britain. In 1888 a beautiful ⅛th scale working steam-model of 4-4-0T No. 60 was built by the North London Railway at its Bow works. Its full-size prototype was completed there in the same year, being one of a numerous class that was the first of the company to be provided with cabs for the enginemen. It had 17in. × 20in. cylinders, 5ft 5in. coupled wheels, 2ft 9½in. bogie wheels, and weighed 46 tons in working order. Eventually it became No. 6491 of the London Midland & Scottish Railway and was broken up at Crewe in 1929.

The model, complete in every detail, is undoubtedly one of the most perfect ever made in the nineteenth century. It is finished in the later style of North London livery, black lined yellow, red and pale blue, and embellished with the company's armorial device. Its equipment includes a full set of detachable destination-boards lettered BROAD STREET, RICHMOND, HIGH BARNET, POTTERS BAR and other places served by North London trains in the past.

After being shown at the Paris Exhibition of 1889 it was put on display at Broad Street station, the company's headquarters. In the base of its showcase was an electric motor and the insertion of a penny in the slot provided, brought all eight wheels into motion. Save for the intervention of World War II, when the model was stored at Crewe for safety, it remained at Broad Street, helping to swell the funds of the Railway Benevolent Institution, until the 1960s, when it was added to the collection of models in the Museum of British Transport.

Photo: Andrew Dow

France. Jean-Francois Cail et Cie of Paris built a conventional low, sleek, double-framed Crampton (2-2)-2-0 locomotive for the Paris–Lyon Railway in 1857. It became No. 22 *La Belgique* of the Paris, Lyon & Mediterranean and in 1869 was sold to the Eastern (Chemin de Fer de l'Est) to become No. 604. Its appearance was radically changed in 1889 when it was rebuilt at the Est Epernay works with a full cab and an experimental twin-drum Flaman boiler and, having lost its name, was nicknamed the *Camel*. In the same year it was put on show at the Paris Exposition after which, during trials on the PLM, it is claimed to have set up a world speed record of 89.9 mph near Pont-sur-Yonne. In its rejuvenated form No. 604 had 6ft 11in. driving-wheels, 15¾in. × 23½in. cylinders, a working-pressure of 162lb./in.² and a tractive effort of 11,100lb. Its weight in working order was 41¾ tons. It was first employed on expresses between Paris (Est) and Belfort, and subsequently on light duties in the Reims area. When it was scrapped around the end of World War I it was one of the last Cramptons in service anywhere.

Dennis Allenden's superb 1/43.5 scale model of this extraordinary-looking engine runs on 1¼in. gauge track and is powered by a Pittman DC66 motor fitted vertically in the firebox. It has been modelled in the final state of about 1900. All external detail has been reproduced, including full cab fittings. The tender is a replica of an Est 10 cubic-metre four-wheeled pattern and, in accordance with contemporary practice, carries its own number. The finish is black, lined with red, the inscriptions, such as the *Chalons-sur-Marne* shed indication on the cab-side, being white, shaded red. The leading buffer-beam is red, lined white, with white inscriptions. The engine number-plate at the base of the chimney and the tender number are of polished bronze; other unpainted metal is polished.
Photo: Dennis Allenden

Mexico. This ⅛th scale-model of Fairlie locomotive No. 41 of the 4ft 8½in. gauge Mexican Railway was lent by Lt. Col J. P. Kennedy, North British Locomotive Co. and Metropolitan-Vickers Electrical Co. to the Science Museum. It is partly cut away on one side to show the internal layout.

The Mexican favoured Fairlies, all 0-6-6-0s. No. 41 was built by Neilson & Co. in 1889. Its power bogies each consisted of two cylinders 16in. × 22in. and six coupled wheels 3ft 6in. in diameter. At 90 per cent of the boiler-pressure of 165lb./in.² the tractive effort was 39,800lb. Heating-surface of the double-ended boiler was 1,532 sq. ft. Its inner firebox was double, with two firing-doors on one side, the combined heating-surface being 180 sq. ft and the grate-area 33 sq. ft. The steam regulators were coupled and operated by a double-ended lever on top of the firebox, so that they could be controlled by either the driver or fireman, who were on opposite sides of the cab.

As the fuel used was chiefly wood, the chimneys were fitted with spark-arresters. The fuel was carried in the 300 cu-ft capacity bunkers above the side tanks which, with the small connecting-tanks beneath the footplates, held 2,850 gallons of water. No. 41 weighed 98 tons in working order, could haul 300 tons up a 1 in 25 gradient and negotiate a curve of 330ft radius.
Photo: Science Museum, London

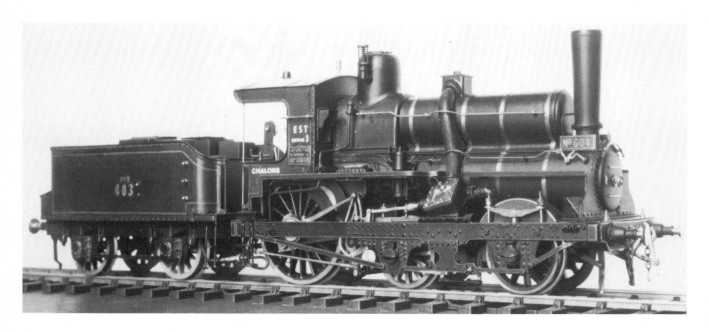

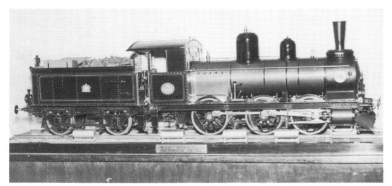

Sweden. The first of the numerous Kd 0-6-0 goods engines of the Swedish State Railways appeared in 1890, being built by Nydqvist & Holm. It was a straightforward design, but proved to be somewhat heavy on coal. Outside cylinders $16\frac{7}{10}$in. × 22in. were provided with inside steam-chests and balanced slide-valves actuated by Allan link motion. Coupled wheels were 4ft $6\frac{1}{2}$in. and the boiler-pressure 143–157lb./in.[2] The heating surface was 1,020 sq. ft and the grate-area $17\frac{1}{5}$ sq. ft. In working order the weight of engine and tender was a little over 60 tons.

No. 701 of the class, the subject of the fine model in the Swedish Railway Museum, was built in 1901 by Falun Wagon & Machine Works. The model itself was made to $\frac{1}{10}$th-scale in 1933 by the SJ workshops at Örebro.
Photo: Swedish Railway Museum, Gävle

Switzerland. In the Swiss Transport Museum the North Eastern Railway (Nordostbahn), which became part of the Swiss Federal system in 1901, is represented by this little 2-4-0 No. 1166. It was made to $\frac{1}{10}$th scale in the railway apprentices' workshop at Zurich during the years 1910–1920.

On the North Eastern the tradition of domeless steam-locomotives became as deeply entrenched as on the Hull & Barnsley Railway of England. No. 1166 was one of a class (B2/3) developed from a domeless 0-4-0 design which was employed on stopping passenger trains in the 1870s. It was built in 1892, as a two-cylinder compound for the same kind of work as its progenitor, by the Swiss Locomotive Works at Winterthur. The high-pressure cylinder was $15\frac{7}{10}$in. × $24\frac{4}{5}$in., the low-pressure $22\frac{1}{2}$in. × $24\frac{4}{5}$in. and the coupled wheels 5ft $2\frac{2}{5}$in. A Bissel truck was provided for the leading pair of carrying-wheels. The rating was about 550 hp and the maximum speed 55 kmph. In working order the total weight was some 58–60 tons, of which 26–27 tons were adhesive.
Photo: Swiss Transport Museum

U.S.A. This impressive ¾in. to 1ft scale-model of a Terre Haute & Indianapolis Railroad 4-6-0 passenger locomotive is, most unexpectedly, to be found in the Royal Scottish Museum in Edinburgh. Also, unusually for an American, it is finished in a livery of brown, lined black and vermilion, with headlamp, pilot and cowcatcher painted the latter colour. It was acquired by the Museum in 1929 from its maker Adam Gilbert of Wallsend-on-Tyne.

The prototype of the model was built in 1893 by the Pittsburgh Locomotive Works (No. 1450). Before entering the service of the railway company, in whose books it became No. 34, it was exhibited with three other locomotives of the same builder at the World's Columbian Exposition in Chicago in 1893, the first Chicago World's Fair. It was designed to haul 565 tons at 40 mph on level track but, with its 6ft coupled wheels, it possessed a higher turn of speed. The cylinders were 20in. × 26in. and the total heating-surface 2,236 sq. ft. Overall, the locomotive and double-bogie tender measured 61ft 6½in. and their combined weight in working order was a little over 95 tons, the weight available for adhesion being 49 tons.

Photo: Royal Scottish Museum, Edinburgh

Britain. Amongst a collection of engineering models presented to the Yorkshire town of Bingley in 1944 by W. H. Smith, a local resident, and displayed in the Central Library there, is an excellent working replica of Midland 4-4-0 No. 2199. The plate on the leading splasher where, strictly speaking, the railway company's heraldic device should be emblazoned, indicates that it was made by H. Skelton of Guildford. The date of construction is not known, nor the significance of the legend 'Faulkner, 95 Shaftesbury Avenue, Piccadilly' on the plate below the smokebox. Yet, despite these minor divergences from full-size practice (sans serif instead of serif numerals on the cabside is another), this 1in. to 1ft scale-model exemplifies all the loveliness of line, proportion and livery that Midland engines of Johnson's design invariably possessed.

The prototype of No. 2199 was built by Sharp Stewart & Co., one of a batch of 20 (Nos. 2183–2202) completed in 1892. The coupled wheels were 7ft $\frac{1}{2}$in., the cylinders 18$\frac{1}{2}$in. × 26in., the total heating-surface 1,223 sq. ft and the working-pressure 160lb./in.^{2} The drumhead, flush smokebox was of the same pattern Johnson had introduced on his immortal single-driver engines in 1887. No. 2199 became No. 419 under the Midland renumbering scheme of 1907 and for many years was stationed at Bedford.
Photo: R. R. Patchett

Britain. Contractor's locomotives often lead a nomadic existence and *Lord Mayor*, a diminutive 0-4-0 saddle tank built in 1893 by Hudswell Clarke & Co. of Leeds (No. 402), worked in a variety of places during its active career. These ranged from Salford Docks and the construction of the G.W.R. Castle Cary—Langport and Tyseley—Henley-in-Arden lines, to the demolition of the Liverpool Overhead Railway, which was its last job. It is now to be seen on the Keighley & Worth Valley Railway, on loan from the Middleton Railway.

It was typical of its kind. Cylinders were 10in. × 16in. and the coupled wheels 2ft 9in. spaced at 5ft 6in. centres. With a working-pressure of 140lb./in.² the tractive effort was 5,750lb. Carrying $\frac{1}{4}$ ton of coal and 400 gallons of water, *Lord Mayor* weighed only 15$\frac{3}{4}$ tons. The immaculate model of this locomotive was made in 1950 to a scale of 1$\frac{1}{16}$in. to 1ft on a gauge of 5in. by Peter Dupen, President of the Romford Model Engineering Club. It won the Championship Cup of the *Model Engineer* Exhibition of that year.
Photo: E. Roddis

U.S.S.R. A strong atmosphere of Tsarist Russia pervades this striking scale-model 4-6-0. The chimney, the generous cab with its doors opening on to the running-plate, and the deck-type handrails all exemplify characteristics of the Russian locomotive of the years before the 1914–1918 war. One has had glimpses of its like in recent films, notably *Dr Zhivago* and *Nicholas and Alexandra*.

In 1892 the Vladikavkaz Railway in south-east Russia ordered six 4-6-0 locomotives, Nos. P41–P46, from the then Kolomna Machine Building Works. They were two-cylinder compounds, with Joy's link-motion and 6ft coupled wheels. The high-pressure cylinder was 19$\frac{3}{5}$in. × 25$\frac{1}{2}$in. and the low-pressure 27$\frac{9}{10}$in. × 25$\frac{1}{2}$in. The boiler-pressure was 162lb./in.² and there was 1,528$\frac{2}{5}$ sq. ft of heating-surface and 19$\frac{9}{10}$ sq. ft of grate-area. The designed speed was 100 kmph. These engines were so successful that more were built, with some detail modifications, at the Kolomna, Sormovsk, Kharkov and Lugansk works up to 1907. Others, fitted for oil burning, were constructed by the Linden Locomotive works of Hanover, Germany.

The model is of the original engine and, despite the absence of its six-wheeled tender, is probably one of the best in the USSR Railways Museum. It was made in 1894, to $\frac{1}{10}$th scale, in the main shops of the Vladikavkaz Railway. The No. P41 is carried at the base of the chimney. Centrally on the boiler is a nameplate with the legend *S.I.Kerbedz*, otherwise Stanislav Ippolitovitch Kerbedz, one-time leading light of the Vladikavkaz Railway Society.
Photo: USSR Railways

France. There was a time when the French State Railway (Chemin de Fer de l'Etat) adopted the reprehensible practice followed by some British railways of naming engines after places in the areas served. Inevitably some such places were of little importance to the outside world, which explains why Etat locomotive No. 2616 was named the gloriously euphonious *St Jean d'Angely*. It was one of a series of 19 2-4-2 express locomotives fitted with Bonnefond valve-gear and built by Cail et Cie of Denain in 1893. Bonnefond valve-gear embodied double inlet-valves and independent inlet and exhaust controls, the motion approximating to the Corliss and similar gears used on stationary engines. Nos. 2602–2620, which formed the series, were the last locomotives to be fitted with this type of valve-gear.

The locomotives were employed to haul Paris–Chartres–Bordeaux expresses. Their cylinders were $17\frac{2}{5}$in. $\times$ $27\frac{7}{10}$in., coupled wheels 6ft 8in. and working-pressure 200lb./in.² The total heating-surface was $1,294\frac{3}{5}$ sq. ft and the grate-area $20\frac{4}{5}$ sq. ft. Weight in working order was 46 tons, with 28 tons 9 cwt available for adhesion. Tenders were non-standard; Nos. 2602–2610 were fitted with tenders from old Orleans–Chartres 2-4-0s and the rest had new tenders built to the same design.

Dennis Allenden's 1/43.5 scale-model of *St Jean d'Angely* portrays the locomotive in 1908 condition, bearing the shed indication *La Roche-sur-Yon* on the cab-sides. It operates on $1\frac{1}{4}$in. gauge track, being powered with a CCW motor actuating the rear coupled axle, which has $\frac{3}{32}$in. of vertical movement, controlled by coil springs. The livery is plain black with polished bands and bronze *Etat* and number on the leading buffer-beam. The chimney number plates, name plates, and builder's plates are engraved.
Photo: Dennis Allenden

U.S.A. No. 999 of the New York Central & Hudson River Railroad is representative of the final development of the American type 4-4-0. It was designed by William Buchanan of the railway company and built at West Albany in 1893. It is claimed that on 10 May of the same year No. 999, hauling the *Empire State Express*, attained a speed of $112\frac{1}{2}$ mph between Batavia and Buffalo. The track joining these two places is level and nearly straight for 36 miles.

The locomotive weighed only 62 tons. The cylinders were 19in. $\times$ 24in., the coupled wheels 7ft 2in. and the boiler-pressure 180lb./in.² Its clean lines, for an American engine, are apparent from the $\frac{1}{4}$in. to 1ft scale model illustrated.
Photo: Smithsonian Institution, Washington

Britain. No Locomotive Superintendent can have carried out more experiments in compounding with so little success than F. W. Webb, who ruled at the Crewe works of the London & North Western Railway with ever-increasing autocracy from 1871 to 1903. The model is of his 2-2-2-2 three-cylinder compound No. 526 *Scottish Chief*, one of the *Greater Britain* class of ten which were built in 1891–1894. It was made to a scale of $\frac{3}{4}$in. to 1ft by S. Smith of Newcastle-upon-Tyne and presented by him to that city's Museum of Science & Engineering.

These engines had a low-pressure 30in. $\times$ 24in. cylinder between the frames and high-pressure 15in. $\times$ 24in. cylinders outside. The 7ft 1in. driving-wheels were not coupled, the leading pair being actuated by the low-pressure cylinder and the trailing pair by the high-pressure cylinders, hence the notation 2-2-2-2. The boiler-pressure was 175lb./in.² and the tubes in the long boiler were divided into two lengths by a

so-called combustion chamber. The total heating-surface was 1,505 $\frac{7}{10}$ sq. ft, made up of 1,346 sq. ft by the tubes, 39 $\frac{7}{10}$ sq. ft by the combustion chamber and 120 $\frac{3}{5}$ sq ft by the firebox. The grate-area amounted to 20$\frac{1}{2}$ sq. ft.

The *Greater Britain* engines, which weighed operationally only 52 $\frac{1}{10}$ tons, and those of the *John Hick* class which followed them, were the only British express tender locomotives to have two driving-axles placed between single leading and trailing carrying axles.

Photo: Museum of Science & Engineering, Newcastle-upon-Tyne

South Africa. The Nederlandsche Zuid-Afrikaansche Spoorweg-Maatschappij, or ZASM, to give its abbreviated title, served the Transvaal and its first section was opened in 1891. Many of its locomotives were supplied by Emil Kessler of Esslingen, Germany. The model exemplifies a typical Kessler engine, 0-6-4 tank No. 4 built in 1894. It was made to a scale of 7mm. to 1ft by the META consortium in 1951–1952 and is to be seen in the Railway Museum, Johannesburg.

Prototype No. 4 was one of a numerous class weighing 45$\frac{3}{4}$ tons in working order and so designated '46 tonner'; they became class B of the South African Railways. Their cylinders were 16$\frac{15}{16}$ in. $\times$ 24$\frac{13}{16}$ in. and coupled wheels 4ft 3$\frac{9}{16}$ in. With a boiler-pressure of 160lb./in.^{2} the tractive effort was 16,580lb. There was 936$\frac{1}{5}$ sq. ft of heating-surface and 15$\frac{3}{5}$ sq. ft of grate-area. The coal bunker held 4 tons and the tanks 1,503 gallons of water. Some of these little engines are still at work in the service of industrial concerns.

Photo: SAR Publicity & Travel Department

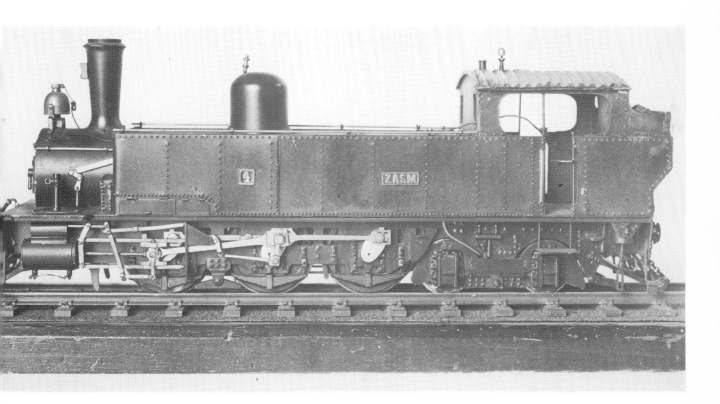

Britain. A numerous locomotive class of the Lancashire & Yorkshire Railway was the 0-6-0 goods engine, with round-top firebox, designed by John (later Sir John) Aspinall, the company's Chief Mechanical Engineer. There were 484 of them. They were compact engines, with 18in. × 26in. cylinders, 5ft 1in. coupled wheels and a boiler-pressure of 160lb./in.² Their total heating-surface was 1,210 sq. ft and grate-area 18¾ sq. ft. With their tenders they weighed a little over 68½ tons in working order.

No. 1249, built in August 1894, was selected by Twining Models Ltd as the prototype for a beautiful non-working 1in. to 1ft scale-model made by them in 1921 for publicity purposes. It was probably one of the finest model locomotives ever produced by this firm. All the motion, outside coupling-rods, buffer-heads, screw-couplings, wheel-treads and other steel parts were in dull nickel plate which, with the semi-gloss of the black paintwork, lined red and white, presented an excellent finish.

The greatest joy to behold was the cab. All the fittings were faithfully reproduced in miniature, the brasswork of the prototype being simulated by electroplating in gold.

Photo: Bassett-Lowke Ltd

U.S.A. Electric locomotive No. 1 of the Baltimore & Ohio Railroad, modelled here on a scale of ¾in. to 1 ft, enjoys some historic significance. It was the first electric-locomotive to be operated on an American main-line railway and was employed on the 3¾ mile-long tunnel-line in Baltimore, where steam engines could not be used because of the fumes. Here it demonstrated some of the potentialities of main-line electrification.

American Locomotive Co. and General Electric built No. 1 in 1895. A single motor was mounted on each axle with a quill drive, and there were no gears. The locomotive was carried on 5ft 2in. wheels and operated on 600 volts DC. It had a horse-power of 1,440 and weighed 96 tons. Taken out of traffic in 1912, it was still used occasionally in the 1920s.

Photo: Smithsonian Institution, Washington

Italy. This model of a typical Italian locomotive of the late Victorian era was made to a scale of $\frac{1}{20}$th, maker and date unknown, and is to be seen in the Museo Nazionale della Scienza e della Tecnica Leonardo da Vinci. It depicts one of a class of fourteen 4-4-0s built in 1896 and 1898 by Ernesto Breda of Milan for the Adriatic Railways, Nos. 1847–1860. Four more, Nos. 1861–1864 were turned out by Costruzioni Meccaniche Saronno in 1898.

These engines became Nos. 5501–5518 of the Italian State Railways when the Adriatic system was taken over in 1905. The model therefore represents the first of the class. The two cylinders were $18\frac{1}{10}$in. $\times$ $23\frac{3}{5}$in., the coupled wheels 5ft $5\frac{1}{2}$in. and the boiler-pressure 170lb./in.^{2} The heating-surface amounted to 1,157 sq. ft and the grate-area to $21\frac{4}{5}$ sq. ft. Operational weight of engine and tender was 70 tons. For the whole of their lives the locomotives worked on the Po valley main lines, Milan–Bologna and Milan–Venice, the last survivors being withdrawn in the 1930s.
Photo: Museo Nazionale della Scienza e della Tecnica Leonardo da Vinci, Milan

Germany. Krauss & Co. of Munich built some class E1 2-8-0 freight locomotives for the Royal Bavarian State Railways in 1896. This was seven years before the first engines of that wheel-arrangement appeared in Britain. The series is portrayed in the Nürnberg Verkehrsmuseum by a $\frac{1}{10}$th scale-model of No. 2054.

These engines had a tractive effort of 19,800lb. Their cylinders were $20\frac{1}{2}$in. $\times$ 22in., the coupled wheels 3ft $3\frac{3}{5}$in. and the working-pressure 176lb./in.^{2} The heating-surface and grate-area were 1,720 and 25 sq. ft respectively. On the Deutsche Reichsbahn they became class 56.3.
Photo: Verkehrsmuseum, Nürnberg

Hungary. An unusual model locomotive in the Budapest Museum of Communication is this 0-8-4 tank made to $\frac{1}{5}$th scale in the Miskolc repair-shops in 1900. It is a splendidly detailed miniature reproduction of class T.IVb (later series 41) rack and adhesion locomotive No. 4281 built at Florids-dorf in 1896 for the Hungarian State Railways.

No. 4281 had four cylinders, two 19$\frac{3}{8}$in. × 19$\frac{3}{8}$in. outside for normal operation and two 15$\frac{1}{2}$in. × 17$\frac{7}{10}$in. for the rack-rail mechanism. Coupled wheels were 3ft 5$\frac{3}{10}$in. and the tractive effort 30,800lb. The heating-surface amounted to 1,785 sq. ft and the grate-area to 25 sq. ft. With a full load of 1,900 gallons of water and 4 tons of coal the operational weight was 70$\frac{1}{2}$ tons.
Photo: Museum of Communication, Budapest

Sweden. A $\frac{1}{10}$th scale-model of Swedish State Railways class Cc 4-4-0 passenger engine No. 463 made in 1927 in the Örebro workshops of the administration. Nydqvist & Holm built the prototype in 1896. The first ten were given narrow cabs but subsequent locomotives had broad cabs with one-piece side-sheets and a front shelter to the tender as illustrated.

The coupled wheels were 6ft 2in., the cylinders 16$\frac{3}{10}$in. × 22in. and the boiler-pressure 157lb./in.² (143lb. in the first ten of the series). The heating-surface was 1,160 sq. ft and the grate-area 21$\frac{1}{2}$ sq. ft. Operational weight was 40 tons 9 cwt.
Photo: Swedish Railway Museum, Gävle

Britain. One of the hard-worked coin-in-the-slot scale-model London & North Western locomotives in the Great Hall at old Euston was of 4-4-0 No. 1901 *Jubilee*. It was made at Crewe works to a scale of $\frac{3}{4}$in. to 1ft early in the present century, it is believed, and is now in the safekeeping of the Museum of British Transport.

Its prototype had also been built at Crewe, in 1897, originally as a four-cylinder simple No. 1501 *Iron Duke* for comparison with the 39 others of the class, which was yet another unsuccessful compound design by F. W. Webb. After conversion to four-cylinder compound it was re-numbered and renamed and the whole batch became known as the *Jubilee* class. As a compound *Jubilee* had outside high-pressure cylinders 15in. × 24in. and inside low-pressure cylinders 19$\frac{1}{2}$in. × 24in., the valve-gear being Joy's. The coupled wheels were 7ft 1in. and the working-pressure 200lb./in.² The boiler had 1,401 sq. ft of heating-surface and the grate area was 20$\frac{1}{2}$ sq. ft. Total operational weight of engine and tender was 81$\frac{1}{2}$ tons.
Photo: London Midland & Scottish Railway

Britain. Of the several first-class scale-models that have been made of Patrick Stirling's famous 8ft single for the Great Northern Railway, one of the best is to be seen in the Royal Scottish Museum in Edinburgh. It is also of special interest because it was built during 1884–1886, only a few years after the appearance of its prototype. Its builder was R. A. Illingworth, who adopted the scale of 1in. to 1ft. The model locomotive and tender measure 4ft 2⅜in. in length over buffers.

The full-size No. 550 emerged from Doncaster works in 1878, the 25th of a series of 53 engines. The driving-wheels were, to be strictly accurate, 8ft 1in. in diameter, the cylinders being 18in. × 28in. and the boiler pressure 140lb./in.^{2} The heating-surface amounted to 1,615 sq. ft and the grate-area to 17⅗ sq. ft. The tender, rather large in comparison with the engine, held 3½ tons of coal and 2,700 gallons of water. Locomotive and tender together weighed a little under 65 tons.

Up to 1881 slotted driving-wheel splashers were provided, but in the course of time these were closed with thin plates. No. 664 was turned out with plain splashers with, fixed centrally, large oval building-plates, of which the model of No. 550 carries small replicas.

Photo: Royal Scottish Museum, Edinburgh

PLATE III

France. English locomotives exhibited in Paris in 1889 resulted in some temporary Anglicisation of certain French engines. This was exemplified by the batch of 0-6-0 goods locomotives Nos 2245–2269 built in 1891 by Société des Batignolles of Paris for the Western Railway (Chemin de Fer de l'Ouest).

These engines had two cylinders 18in. × 25in., the valve-gear being Walschaerts, which actuated inclined slide-valves. The coupled wheels were 4ft 8in. and the boiler-pressure 147lb./in.² The tractive effort was 20,900lb. and the weight ready for service 36¾ tons.

After the merger of the Western and State (Chemin de Fer de l'Etat) systems in 1909 the locomotives were renumbered and some were transferred to the Loire valley area. All 25

were still at work in 1938, to become French Railways (SNCF) class 030-D, and in 1950 those that remained were shedded at Dol-de-Bretagne for working trains in Brittany and Normandy.

Dennis Allenden's beautiful model of the class is of No. 2247, in post-1909 condition as Etat 030–863, with the addition of Westinghouse brake for passenger-train operation. It is made to 1/43.5 scale, 1¼in. gauge. On the cab side is the legend *Fougeres*, indicating the place at which the prototype was shedded. The tender is the standard Ouest 8 cubic-metre pattern, which the class retained most of their working lives.

Photo: Dennis Allenden

PLATE IV

U.S.A. The urge to model can sometimes be very strong, as in this case. The prototype consisted of the remains of a pigmy nineteenth-century American narrow-gauge industrial 0-4-0 saddle tank locomotive, which had survived in Coultersville, California. Weighing a mere eight tons, it had been built by the H. K. Porter Co. of Pittsburgh in 1896 for the Merced Gold Mining Co. It spent all its active life in the mountains, trundling gold ore over the four miles of 2ft gauge iron from the Mary Harrison mine to the Potosi mill. Then in 1904 it was abandoned and forgotten until some time after 1933, when it was rescued and brought into nearby Coultersville.

Edward Groth of Scottsdale, Arizona, photographed what was left of the old engine a few years ago. He measured it and established its wheelbase of 4ft, length of 16ft 11in. over couplers and other vital statistics, such as 2ft coupled wheels and 7in. × 12in. cylinders. Much of its enchantment must have remained, for he decided to construct a working model of it in HO scale to fine standards. This entailed making the motor as well, to fit into the shape of the saddle tank. It took three years to complete from scratch. It is almost entirely made of brass, but the pilot-beam and footboards are of walnut. The spark-arrester mesh in the chimney is stainless steel silk-screen material. The cab fittings include firehole door and latch, trycocks, regulator, steam-gauge, operable brake, injector, blower and steam valves; there are oil-cans and a rack to hold them.

The minute size of this exquisite model, the smallest in this book, may be judged by its comparison with a silver dollar, the photograph being taken before painting was carried out. Deservedly it was awarded first prize for steam-locomotives and best of show at the Pacific Coast Convention of the National Model Railroad Association in 1971.
Photo: Edward Groth

South Africa. The 6th-class 4-6-0 locomotives of the Cape Government Railways were not only good-lookers, especially those with bogie tenders, but were in every way a successful design. The first appeared in 1893 and the last in 1901. Some are still at work today, with over 70 years to their credit, a distinction which it is doubtful any other class elsewhere in the world can claim.

No. 202, represented by the 7mm. to 1ft scale-model made by the META consortium in 1951–1952, was one of a batch of 50 built by Neilson Reid & Co. in 1897, becoming class 6B of the South African Railways. Cylinders were 17in. × 26 in., coupled wheels 4ft 6in. and working-pressure 160 lb./in.², at 75 per cent of which the tractive effort was 16,690 lb. Heating-surface totalled 1,116 sq. ft and the grate-area $16\frac{3}{5}$ sq. ft. The bogie tender held $5\frac{1}{2}$ tons of coal and 2,600 gallons of water, making the operational weight of engine and tender $80\frac{3}{4}$ tons. The model is to be seen in the Railway Museum, Johannesburg.
Photo: SAR Publicity & Travel Department

Holland. The prototype of this pretty little 4-4-0 suburban tank engine No. 41 of the Netherlands Central Railway was constructed by Richard Hartmann of Chemnitz in 1899. Its coupled wheels were 4ft $5\frac{1}{8}$in., cylinders $14\frac{3}{4}$in. × $19\frac{3}{4}$in. and boiler-pressure 175lb./in.² The grate-area was 11 sq. ft and the total heating-surface 698 sq. ft. Its tanks and bunker held $3\frac{1}{2}$ cu.m of coal and 1,000 kg of water. In working order the weight was 37.100 kg. Further engines of the class, of generally similar dimensions, were built during the years 1901–1903 by Hartmann and by the Hohenzollern Works of Dusseldorf.

Utrecht Railway Museum displays the model, which was made to $\frac{1}{10}$th scale by the apprentices' department of the main repair-shop of the Netherlands Railway at Haarlem in 1956–1957. It is finished in the distinctive Netherlands Central livery of yellow ochre, elaborately lined-out and exactly the same as the Stroudley livery for the London, Brighton & South Coast Railway. Much polished brass-work is also in evidence.
Photo: Railway Museum, Utrecht

Britain. John Aspinall's class 1400 inside-cylinder Atlantics, introduced in 1899, were the leading express engines of the Lancashire & Yorkshire Railway for the ensuing decade. Forty were built up to 1902 and one of them, No. 737, was the first British locomotive to be fitted with a low-degree superheater. When they first appeared they had the largest boilers in the country. Carried between 7ft 3in. coupled wheels (which were exceeded only by those of 7ft 7¼in. of two North Eastern 4-4-0s), these boilers, of 4ft 9in. minimum diameter, 17ft 1⅜in. long and pitched with their centres 8ft 11in. above the rails, gave the engines a rather clumsy look, but they did the job they were designed to do. The total heating-surface was 2,052⅛ sq. ft, to which the Belpaire firebox contributed 175⅛ sq. ft. The grate-area was 26 sq. ft.

Joy valve-gear operated the valve-chests above the 19in. × 26in. cylinders and the working-pressure was 175lb./in.² The tenders, which were fitted with water pick-up gear, held 2,290 gallons of water and 5 tons of coal. In working order locomotive and tender weighed 89⅝ tons. The model of No. 1400 is in the Museum of British Transport. It was made to a scale of ¾in. to 1ft by Crewe Apprentices School in 1960, and its splendid external detail includes full cab-fittings.

Photo: Andrew Dow

France. The first American locomotives to be imported into France were 11 express 4-4-0s built in 1899 by Baldwin Locomotive Works. They were ordered by the State Railway (Chemin de Fer de l'Etat) and allotted Nos. 2801–2805 and 2851–2856, the first batch being Vauclain compounds and the second simples. In all other respects the two batches were identical, save only as regards No. 2805 *Montlieu*, which was provided with a Baldwin bogie tender, doubtless because it was exhibited at the Paris Exposition of 1900. The others had standard Etat tenders, originally four-wheeled and latterly bogie.

The high- and low-pressure cylinders of the compounds were located one above the other, in the usual Vauclain style, and actuated a common crosshead and connecting-rod; they therefore required only two sets of valve-gear, in this case Stephenson, with piston valves. The high-pressure cylinders were 13in. and the low-pressure 22in. in diameter, the stroke being 26in. The cylinders of the simple engines were 17¼in. × 26in. Boilers were 4ft 10in. diameter and 12ft 1in. long, with a working-pressure of 215lb./in.² Total heating-surface was 1,892⅔ sq. ft and the grate-area 25⅔ sq. ft. Operational weight of the engine was 52 tons 13 cwt, with 31 tons 3 cwt available for the adhesion of the 7ft coupled wheels.

These locomotives were originally employed on express services Paris (Montparnasse)–Chartres–Thouars, but after 1905 were demoted to semi-fast services on the lines in the Loire valley and on the Atlantic coast. The last was scrapped in 1932. The whole class had been renumbered in 1909, when No. 2804, the subject of Dennis Allenden's craftsmanship, became No. 220–804. His model is shown with the new number displayed on the horizontal centre-line of the boiler, instead of in the former position each side of the base of the chimney, with the nameplate *Richelieu* retained on each leading splasher.

Built to a scale of 1/43.5, 1¼in. gauge, No. 220–804 is finished in dark olive green, with polished brass bands and plates, and black smokebox, chimney, wheels and chassis. The tender is a replica of that shown with sister engine No. 2805 at the Paris Exposition.

Photo: Dennis Allenden

Britain. Among the most useful of all London & South Western locomotives were the class T9 4-4-0s, designed by the company's Mechanical Engineer, Dugald Drummond, and nicknamed *Greyhounds*. They also enjoyed strong aesthetic appeal, due to simplicity of outline, good proportions and a lovely livery. The latter was officially described as royal green, edged with purple brown having an inner black band lined white on either side. Despite the small scale of 7mm to 1ft to which the accompanying reproduction of No. 702 was built, its faultless craftsmanship and finish recreate all the characteristics of Drummond's design more convincingly than any other model known to the author. It was made in 1965 by J. S. Beeson of Ringwood.

No. 702 was the first of the initial batch of 30 constructed by Dübs & Co., Nos. 702–719 and 721–732, in 1899–1900. The cylinders were $18\frac{1}{2}$in. × 26in. and the coupled wheels 6ft 7in. The boiler had a length of 10ft 6in. and diameter of 4ft 5in. and the working-pressure was 175lb./in.². The grate-area was 24 sq. ft and the heating surface was made up of $1,186\frac{2}{5}$ sq. ft by the tubes, $148\frac{3}{10}$ sq. ft by the firebox and 165 sq. ft by the firebox water-tubes, these last being a Drummond innovation.

Originally the T9s were provided with six-wheeled tenders, which made their operational weight 88 tons 16 cwt, but in a few years attractive bogie tenders, holding 4,000 gallons of water and 4 tons of coal, took their place. The working order weight was thus increased to 92 tons 19 cwt. Superheating gave the T9s a new lease of life and all 66, of which the class finally consisted, entered British Railways stock. Withdrawal began in 1950 and No. 702 (then No. 30702) was taken out of service in 1959. Last to go was No. 30120 which, happily, has been preserved.
Photo: J. S. Beeson

Germany. *Dr von Clemm* is undoubtedly the most extraordinary-looking model locomotive in the Nürnberg Verkehrsmuseum. It is a $\frac{1}{10}$th scale replica of a four-coupled engine with a steam-driven leading bogie! Its wheel arrangement is 2-2-2-0-4-2 or, in Continental parlance, 1a1-B1.

The prototype was built by Krauss & Co. in 1900 for the Pfalz Railways and displayed at the Paris Exhibition of the same year. It was a two-cylinder compound with one high-pressure $16\frac{3}{10}$in. × 26in. cylinder and one low-pressure $25\frac{1}{2}$in. × 26in. cylinder, the diameter of the coupled wheels being 5ft $3\frac{3}{10}$in. The bogie wheels were 3ft $3\frac{3}{10}$in. in diameter; the centre pair were flangeless and actuated by $10\frac{1}{2}$in. × $15\frac{7}{10}$ in. cylinders, making it an auxiliary engine somewhat akin to the booster of later years. With a working pressure of 206lb./in.² the tractive power was 11,460lb. There was 2,056 sq. ft of heating-surface and 82 sq. ft of area, the operational weight of engine and tender being 107 tons.

Dr von Clemm was not a success. The centre pair of wheels in the bogie were removed before the Pfalz Railways were absorbed by the Royal Bavarian State Railways in 1909, making it a 4-4-2, and it was taken out of service sometime before 1920.
Photo: Verkehrsmuseum, Nürnberg

Britain. One of the best known locomotives of the Great Eastern Railway was 4-4-0 No. 1900, completed at Stratford works in March 1900 and named *Claud Hamilton* after the chairman of the company. With its white cab-roof, polished brasswork, livery of Royal blue lined black and red, and *bas relief* coat of arms in full colours on the leading splashers, it is not surprising that it won a Grand Prix at the Paris Exhibition of 1900. *Claud Hamilton* was designed by James Holden, the Locomotive Superintendent, and was equipped with his system of oil firing. In consequence, the tender, which held 2,790 gallons of water and 715 of oil, was of distinctive profile, having coping-plates turned inwards instead of outwards.

The coupled wheels were 7ft and the cylinders 19in. × 26in. The boiler, of 4ft 8in. external diameter and 11ft 9in. in length, together with the round-topped firebox 7ft long and 4ft ½in. wide, gave a total heating-surface of 1,630½ sq. ft, the grate-area being a little over 21 sq. ft. The boiler-pressure was 180lb./in.², at 85 per cent of which the tractive effort was 17,100lb. Air-operated reversing gear and water-scoop were provided.

Claud Hamilton was the last passenger engine to use liquid fuel on the Great Eastern, the system being discontinued because of the increasing cost of oil-fuel. In 1925 it was fitted with a Belpaire boiler and higher cab, and eight years later such a major reconstruction took place that little of the original engine remained; even a new nameplate was provided. The locomotive was withdrawn from traffic in May 1947 with a million-and-a-quarter miles to its credit. It is fortunate that posterity can see this beautiful locomotive modelled in the form in which it was originally built. When it was under construction in 1900 a working-model of it was made at Stratford by the late George Perry, who became foreman of the paint-shop. Built to a scale of 1½in. to 1ft, it is now on display in the Museum of Transport.
Photo: Andrew Dow

U.S.A. Around the turn of the century the 4-4-2 or Atlantic was a very popular wheel-arrangement for express passenger locomotives in the United States. Only when steel passenger-cars came on the scene in the early 1900s did the 4-4-2 defer to the heavier and more powerful 4-6-2. Chicago & North Western Railway class D No. 1015 is a typical example of the American Atlantic. It was built in 1900 by the Schenectady Locomotive Works and was to be seen at the head of the *Overland Ltd* express for many years. It had 20in. × 26in. cylinders, 6ft 8in. coupled wheels and a boiler-pressure of 200lb./in.². With its tender its operational weight was 101 tons.

The model is in the Smithsonian Institution. It was made to a scale of ½in. to 1ft by Leo Myers, whose *General* and *Texas* are depicted on earlier pages.
Photo: Smithsonian Institution, Washington

Britain. Sixty class R 4-4-0 express passenger-locomotives were built by the North Eastern Railway, the first batch appearing in 1899 and the last in 1907. Their straightforward, handsome lines, enhanced by a grass-green livery, lined black and white, are captured by this model of No. 2021, which was made to a scale of ¾in. to 1ft by H. P. Jackson of York. It depicts the prototype as originally constructed in 1900, without the customary heraldic device between the words NORTH and EASTERN on the tender. It is to be seen in the Museum of Science & Engineering, Newcastle-upon-Tyne.

Wilson Worsdell was the Locomotive Superintendent

responsible for the class R engines. They enjoyed extreme simplicity of design and, in consequence, were not expensive to maintain. No. 2011 held a mileage record in this respect; in 1902 it ran 125,365 miles without once visiting the repair-shops. Their cylinders were 19in. × 26in. and coupled wheels 6ft 10in., which gave them a good turn of speed. One of the best performances was put up by No. 2020 which, in 1901, took a train from Darlington to York in 41¼ minutes, averaging about 66 mph. Their total heating-surface was 1,527 sq. ft and grate area 20 sq. ft. The working-pressure was 200lb./in.², reduced to 170lb. when superheaters were eventually provided. The tender held 3,537 gallons of water and 5 tons of coal, making the operational weight of the engine and tender 89⅗ tons.

Photo: Museum of Science & Engineering, Newcastle-upon-Tyne

Italy. At the Paris Exhibition of 1900 an experimental four-cylinder compound locomotive of the Italian Southern Railway created a great deal of interest. The cab and firebox were placed at the leading end, with the smokebox and chimney trailing. The coal-bunkers were fixed each side of the firebox and the water was carried in a simple cylindrical tank running on six wheels. By this means Signor Planchar, the railway company's director of locomotive-power, secured the large grate-area of 32 sq. ft and gave the enginemen a fine view of the line ahead. The experiment was so successful that a fleet of these unconventional engines was put to work, the construction being undertaken by the famous German locomotive-builder Borsig of Berlin.

The engines had 6ft 3⅛in. coupled wheels, 14⅛in. × 25½in. high-pressure cylinders and 23¼in. × 25½in. low-pressure cylinders. The heating-surface amounted to 1,650 sq. ft and the boiler-pressure was 213lb./in.² With a full load of 4 tons of coal and 4,400 gallons of water the working-order weight of engine and tender was 106 tons. One coal bunker has been omitted and a short section of the side behind the cab cut away to show the internal arrangement of the firebox and grate in the accompanying photograph. The model is of No. 6702 and was made to ¹⁄₂₀th scale.

Photo: Museo Nazionale della Scienza e della Tecnica Leonardo da Vinci, Milan

Finland. Great Britain, Germany, Switzerland and Finland all constructed class G11 2-6-0 mixed-traffic locomotives for the Finnish State Railways over the years 1892–1905. They are represented by this $\frac{1}{10}$th-scale model made in 1931 by apprentices in Helsinki workshops and now in the Railway Museum at the station there.

No. 400 was one of a batch of 33 turned out by Tampereen Pellava-ja Rauta-Teollisuus Osake-Yhtiö of Finland in 1901–1903. It was a two-cylinder compound, the high-pressure cylinder being $15\frac{3}{4}$in. $\times$ $23\frac{5}{8}$in. and the low-pressure $22\frac{13}{16}$in. $\times$ $23\frac{5}{8}$in. Coupled wheels were 4ft $1\frac{3}{16}$in. and the working-pressure 178lb./in.², giving a tractive effort of 12,700lb. The total heating-surface was 824 sq. ft and the grate-area $14\frac{9}{10}$ sq. ft. In working order engine and tender weighed a little less than 58 tons.
Photo: Finnish State Railways

Hungary. How typically Central European is this striking $\frac{1}{50}$th-scale replica of No. 801 of the Hungarian State Railways. It is another delightful model in the Museum of Communication in Budapest.

The superheated simple-expansion prototype was built in 1901 as class I1, later redesignated class 202. The two cylinders were 20in. $\times$ $26\frac{7}{10}$in., the coupled wheels 6ft $10\frac{3}{8}$in. and the tractive power 14,450lb. The total evaporative heating-surface was 1,547 sq. ft and the grate-area $32\frac{1}{4}$ sq. ft. In working order the engine weighed $62\frac{1}{2}$ tons and the tender $40\frac{1}{4}$ tons, the capacity of the latter being 4,675 gallons of water and seven tons of coal. If there really had been a Ruritania this surely must be the very embodiment of the type of locomotive one would have seen at the head of the express for the capital at Strelsau.
Photo: Museum of Communication, Budapest

New Zealand. Thirteen 4-6-2 locomotives built by the Baldwin Locomotive Works in 1901 for the New Zealand Railways were the first main-line Pacifics in the world. With their wide fireboxes, piston-valves and Walschaerts gear they represented a notable advance in design. They became the second class Q of the NZR. These engines were capable of hauling 600-ton goods trains on the level, or 170 tons up gradients of 1 in 35, and handled passenger trains at speeds up to 50 mph. They had 16in. × 22in. cylinders, 4ft 1⅛in. coupled wheels and a working-pressure of 200lb./in.². Their heating-surface was 1,673 sq. ft and grate-area 40 sq. ft. In working order the engine and tender weighed 72 tons and the last were taken out of service in 1957.

The splendid display model of No. 347 reproduced was made by three craftsmen, the engine by Charles Jonas, the cab-fittings by Frank Roberts and the tender by Foster Clark. Its scale is ½in. to 1ft and the gauge 1¾in.
Photo: New Zealand Railways Publicity & Advertising Dept

France. Some fine four-cylinder 4-6-0 compound locomotives appeared on the Western Railway of France in 1901. The de Glehn system of compounding, as modified by du Bousquet, was adopted, the engines being built in the company's Batignolles works to the designs of M. Clérault. They acquitted themselves well at the head of Paris–Dieppe boat trains. The high-pressure cylinders had a diameter of 14¾in. and low-pressure 21⅜in., both having a stroke of 25⅜in. The coupled wheels were 5ft 6⅖in. and the boiler-pressure 213³⁄₁₀lb./in.². There was a total of 2,280 sq. ft of heating-surface and 26⅞ sq. ft of grate-area. Engine and tender had an operational weight of 99 tons, including 3,300 gallons of water and 5 tons of coal.

P. Regnard of Paris was inspired to make a splendid ¹⁄₁₀th-scale model of No. 2702 of the class in 1903. The left-hand side depicted the external appearance, but the right-hand side was sectionalised and parts cut away so as to show the interior layout. The boiler and firebox were divided longitudinally and the right-hand high-pressure cylinder was shown in section. The model can be put in motion by compressed air, so giving a clear picture of the movements that take place. For many years it has been exhibited in the Science Museum, where the author was thrilled to make his first youthful encounter with it just after World War I.
Photos: Crown Copyright, Science Museum, London

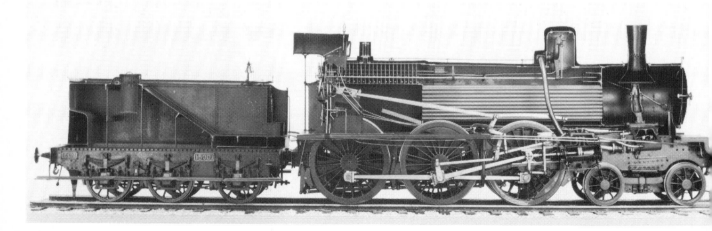

Britain. It is likely that this $1\frac{1}{16}$in. to 1ft, 5in. gauge scale-replica of the former Great Northern Railway Atlantic locomotive No. 295 is the most perfect working model of the class in existence. Its owner, W. A. Carter of Norbury, London, aimed at the construction of a successful working model of the prototype both inside and out. Making all the patterns himself, the task took 14 years and was crowned with success. Completed in 1964, the model won the Championship Cup and J. N. Maskelyne Memorial Cup at the *Model Engineer Exhibition* of that year; the Gold Medal of the Society of Model & Experimental Engineers in 1965; and the Duke of Edinburgh Trophy at the *Model Engineer Exhibition* of 1968.

Apart from the metallic bellows used in the brake-cylinders (because rubber rings get overheated on a model), everything was made by the builder, including pressure- and vacuum-gauges and transfers. An eight-element superheater is fitted to the boiler, which works at a pressure of 90lb./in.² The cylinders are $1\frac{3}{4}$in. $\times$ $2\frac{1}{8}$in., and have the balanced slide-valves of the original. Steam and gravity sanding-gear, fully automatic vacuum-brakes and, most unusually for a model locomotive, carriage steam-warming apparatus, are included in the equipment. Weighing $2\frac{1}{4}$ cwt, this superb model has shown itself capable of hauling loads in excess of half a ton, and has already steamed some 200 miles. It is finished in the condition in which its prototype was running in 1939, hence the livery and number of the LNER.

The full-size locomotive was designed by H. A. Ivatt and built at the Doncaster works of the Great Northern in 1905. Eighty sister engines, beginning with No. 251, made up the class, their construction taking place over the years 1902 to 1908. The boiler, large for its time, had a barrel 16ft $3\frac{7}{8}$in. long with a maximum outside diameter of 5ft 6in.; its working-pressure was 175lb./in.² The wide firebox was of a design then new to Britain. Total evaporative heating-surface was 2,500 sq ft and the grate-area $30\frac{9}{10}$ sq. ft. The two cylinders were $18\frac{3}{4}$in. $\times$ 24in. and the coupled wheels 6ft $7\frac{1}{2}$in. In working order the engine weighed $68\frac{3}{8}$ tons and the tender $40\frac{9}{10}$ tons with its 3,670 gallons of water and 5 tons of coal. These engines put up their finest performances in express passenger-train working after they had been modified by H. N. Gresley, who gave them large superheaters.

Photo: W. A. Carter

Sweden. Introduced in 1902 to meet the need for a modern 0-6-0 shunting tank, the class Ke engines of the Swedish State Railways were also extensively used for suburban traffic, although their highest permissible speed was 39mph. They were, in fact, a tank version of the class Kd 0-6-0 goods locomotives, the coupled wheels 4ft 6½in., cylinders 16 $\frac{7}{10}$ in. × 22in., motion and frames being identical. The heating-surface and grate-area were less, however, at 908 sq. ft and 16$\frac{3}{4}$ sq. ft respectively. Boiler-pressure was 157 lb./in.² and weight in working order 39 tons 17 cwt.

The model of No. 775 illustrated was made to a scale of $\frac{1}{10}$th in the SJ Örebro workshops in 1928. The prototype was built by Ljunggrens of Kristianstad in 1903.
Photo: Swedish Railway Museum, Gävle

South Africa. The first locomotive D. A. Hendrie designed on being appointed Locomotive Superintendent of the Natal Government Railways in 1903 was a 4-8-2 tank, of which 25 were built by the North British Locomotive Co. in the following year. They were allotted Nos. 250–274 and ultimately became class G of the South African Railways. A 7mm. to 1ft scale-model of No. 250 is displayed in the Railway Museum, Johannesburg. It was made by the META consortium in 1951–1952.

These engines weighed a modest 60 tons 6 cwt in working order but developed a tractive effort of 22,280lb. at 75 per cent of the working-pressure of 175lb./in.². Their cylinders were 18in. × 22in. and coupled wheels 3ft 6in. The total heating-surface was 1,223 sq. ft and grate-area 19 sq. ft. The limited coal and water capacity—2½ tons and 1,560 gallons—restricted their range of operation. In their early days they took the corridor trains out of Durban. They ended on shunting duties in SAR yards and on the lines of industrial concerns.
Photo: SAR Publicity & Travel Department

Britain. Oliver Carter, when a plumber in the permanent way department at Darlington, built this striking model of class V North Eastern Atlantic No. 649 to a scale of 1in. to 1ft. It was purchased by the directors of the company and is now displayed in the Railway Museum at York.

The first of the North Eastern Atlantics was No. 532, which emerged from Gateshead Works towards the end of 1903. It was designed by Wilson Worsdell, the Chief Mechanical Engineer. No. 649 followed in 1904, in which year eight more were built. By 1910 there were 20 of them and they all survived to become class C6 of the London & North Eastern Railway. Coupled wheels were 6ft 10in. and the cylinders 20in. × 28in. The boiler had a diameter of 5ft 6in., length of 15ft 10½in. and a working-pressure of 200lb./in.². The total heating-surface was 2,456 sq. ft and there was a grate-area of 27 sq. ft. The tender held 4,125 gallons of water and 5 tons of coal. Engine and tender in working order weighed 115½ tons and measured 62ft 4in. in length. These locomotives did sterling work at the head of East Coast Route expresses, including the *Flying Scotsman*.
Photo: British Railways

Switzerland. Between 1904 and 1909 the Swiss Locomotive Works at Winterthur built some handsome 4-6-0 four-cylinder compounds, known as class A3/5, for the Swiss Federal Railways. The design was a repetition of a successful batch of engines turned out by the same builders in 1902 for the Jura-Simplon Railway (Geneva-Vallorbe-Brigue) which, a year later, became an important part of the Swiss Federal system.

The high-pressure cylinders, 14⅜in. × 26in., were actuated by Walschaerts gear, and the low-pressure, 24½in. × 26in. by Joy's valve-gear. The diameter of the coupled wheels was 5ft 10in. and of the bogie wheels 2ft 9½in. The boiler, which had a working-pressure of 213lb./in.², had the benefit of a total heating-surface of over 1,792 sq. ft, the grate-area being 28 sq. ft. In working order the locomotive and its double bogie tender, which held 3,742 gallons of water and 5 tons of coal, weighed nearly 101½ tons.

When first introduced the class was put to work on the haulage of express passenger-trains on the Geneva-Berne-Olten, Lausanne-Brigue and Basle-Lucerne services. Their maximum speed was 62 mph. The Swiss Transport Museum exhibits the $\frac{1}{10}$th scale-model of No. 748 illustrated. It was made in the apprentices workshop of von Roll'sche Eisenwerke, Gerlafingen in 1946.
Photo: Swiss Transport Museum, Lucerne

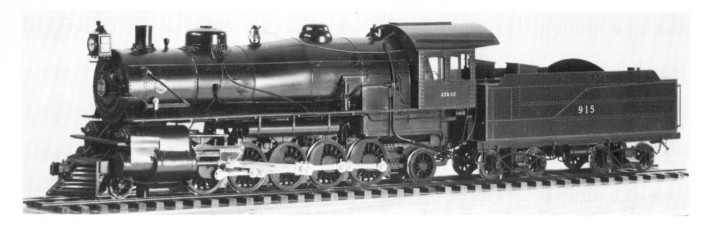

U.S.A. At the time of their construction by Baldwin Locomotive Works in 1904, the seventy 2-10-2 freight engines of the Atchison, Topeka & Santa Fé Railroad were claimed not only to be the most powerful but also the heaviest in the world. With their bogie tenders they weighed just under 201 tons. The 2-10-2 wheel-arrangement was henceforth known as the *Santa Fé*. These immense locomotives were tandem compounds, having on each side a high-pressure 19in. × 32in. cylinder ahead of a low-pressure 32in. × 32in. cylinder on the same centre-line, sharing a common piston-rod and driving the intermediate pair of coupled wheels. This created a rather clumsy looking front-end and caused them to be nicknamed *hogs*.

The diameter of the coupled wheels was 4ft 9in. and that of the leading and trailing pony-trucks 2ft 5¼in. and 3ft 4in. respectively. The tapered boiler had a minimum diameter of 6ft 6¾in. and a working-pressure of 225lb./in.². Total heating-surface was 4,796 sq. ft and the grate-area 58½ sq. ft.

Severn-Lamb Ltd captured all the features of the prototype in the accompanying ½in.-to-1ft reproduction made for the Smithsonian Institution, although when the full-size No. 915 first appeared the company's initials on the cab-side and numerals on the tender were more extended and displayed in larger characters.
Photo: Smithsonian Institution, Washington

South Africa. With the end of the Boer War the Imperial Military Railways, which had assumed control of the Orange Free State and Transvaal systems, were transferred to civil control and set up as the Central South African Railways on 1 July 1902. New engines were urgently needed to make good the casualties of war and, after main-line needs had been met, an order was placed with Vulcan Foundry for eight 4-6-4 tanks for suburban services on the Reef. These were designated class F and went into operation in 1904, being allotted Nos. 260–267, later becoming Nos. 78–85 of the South African Railways.

Cylinders were 18in. × 26in., coupled wheels 4ft 6in. and working-pressure 200lb./in.², which produced a tractive effort of 23,410lb. The total heating-surface was 1,481 sq. ft and the grate-area 21¾ sq. ft. Fully loaded with three tons of coal and 1,800 gallons of water the working order weight was 79 tons. The handsome proportions of these locomotives, which were dubbed *Chocolate Boxes*, are to be seen again in the model of No. 260, exhibited in the Railway Museum at Johannesburg. This was made in 1951–1952 to a scale of 7mm. to 1ft by the META consortium.
Photo: SAR Publicity & Travel Department

Britain. This 1½in. to 1ft scale-model of Cambrian Railways 4-4-0 No. 98 was built at Oswestry workshops, after working hours, by foremen and craftsmen there. The plate beneath the smokebox carries the legend 'Cambrian Railways, makers, 1907'. Its livery is black, lined-out in gamboge edged vermilion, with the Prince of Wales' feathers, the crest of the Cambrian, embellishing the tender sides. The model was presented by British Railways to the National Trust at the end of 1966, and is now to be seen in the Penrhyn Castle Railway Museum, near Bangor, Caernarvonshire, where the photograph was taken.

Its prototype was one of five engines, Nos. 94–98, built in 1904 by Robert Stephenson & Co. (maker's Nos. 3131–3135) for heavy express-train duties. Cylinders were 18½in. × 26in., coupled wheels 6ft, the working-pressure 170lb./in.², the grate-area 20½ sq. ft and the total heating-surface 1,283 sq. ft. With the tender, which held 2,500 gallons of water and 4 tons of coal, the weight in working order was 76½ tons.
Photo: Penrhyn Castle Railway Museum

Britain. The McIntosh 4-4-0s of the Caledonian Railway have had many admirers, but surely none more ardent than the late W. H. Dearden, AMICE. Having spent more than 10,000 hours constructing a ¾in. to 1ft working scale-model of No. 140, he presented it to the Institution of Mechanical Engineers in 1936 and took in hand another, again a working model, which he completed to the scale of 1in. to 1ft. His first model is illustrated. Every part of it he made himself, except only the Caledonian armorial devices, which were manufactured by a jeweller. The cylinders, slide-bars and motion-plate were assembled in auxiliary frames and placed entire between the main frames. Case hardening was applied to parts of the link-motion. He made use of jigs for several details such as hornblocks and axleboxes to ensure accuracy in construction. The model is unpainted, being given a bright finish. The original boiler had a working-pressure of 80lb./in.² and oil was used as the fuel. After a good deal of running on a garden railway, coal replaced the oil and a new boiler with a working-pressure of 130lb./in.² was provided.

McIntosh's 140 class 4-4-0s of 1904 were built for handling express passenger-trains between Carlisle and the North. They were very similar to his previous 900 class, but possessed a large-diameter boiler, a longer firebox and a greater water-capacity in the tender. The cylinders were 19in. × 26in., the coupled wheels 6ft 6in. and the working-pressure 180lb./in.². Weight of engine and tender was nearly 107½ tons, which included 4,300 gallons of water and 4½ tons of coal.
Photo: R. Armitage

Canada. Class F2 4-6-0s Nos. 25, 26 and 27 of the Toronto, Hamilton & Buffalo Railway were built in 1904 by the Locomotive & Machine Co. of Montreal Ltd (later known as the Montreal Locomotive Works), and to No. 25 fell the distinction of being the first engine to be completed by the firm for any customer. The model of this locomotive, built to a scale of ¼in. to 1ft, is owned by Andrew Merrilees of Toronto, who is forming a collection of every single class of TH&B engine.

With 18½in. × 26in. cylinders, 5ft coupled wheels and a working-pressure of 195lb./in.², the F2 locomotives had a tractive effort of 26,820lb. Operationally, they weighed a little under 63 tons. No. 25 was sold in 1926 to Spruce Falls Power & Paper Co. Ltd of Kapuskasing, Ontario, becoming No. 104 of the new owner. It was scrapped about 1954.
Photo: Andrew Merrilees Ltd

Germany. One-man operation, which has come to the fore in bus transport in recent years, was a feature of steam-traction on the Royal Bavarian State Railways as long ago as 1906. In that year the class PtL2/2 0-4-0 locomotive was introduced. It was supplied by Krauss & Co. for services on subsidiary lines and was operated by a driver-fireman.

The $\frac{1}{10}$th scale-model illustrated of No. 4504 reproduces in miniature all the distinctive external features of these diminutive locomotives. Their two cylinders were 12in. $\times$ 15$\frac{7}{10}$in. and the coupled wheels 3ft 3$\frac{3}{8}$in. The total heating-surface was 382 sq. ft and the grate-area 6$\frac{1}{2}$ sq. ft. With a boiler-pressure of 176lb./in.^{2} the tractive power was 9,920lb. Weight in working order was 21$\frac{7}{10}$ tons. These engines became class 98.3 of the Deutsche Reichsbahn upon the formation of the latter in 1920.
Photo: Verkehrsmuseum, Nürnberg

Sweden. A $\frac{1}{10}$th scale-model of class A 4-4-2 No. 1025 of the Swedish State Railways, which was made in the Örebro workshops of the system in 1911. There were 26 of these locomotives, the pioneer being No. 1000, which emerged from the Trollhattan works of Nydqvist & Holm in 1906. The coupled wheels were 6ft 2in., the cylinders 19$\frac{3}{4}$in. $\times$ 23$\frac{5}{8}$in. and the boiler-pressure 170lb./in.^{2}, producing a tractive effort of 13,700lb. A Schmidt superheater with a surface of 353 sq. ft was fitted. The total heating-surface was 1,432 sq. ft and the grate-area 28 sq. ft. In working order the engine weighed nearly 59$\frac{1}{2}$ tons, of which more than half was available for adhesion.

Originally six-wheeled tenders holding 3,080 gallons of water and 4$\frac{1}{2}$ tons of coal were allotted to all locomotives in the class. Within a few years, however, these were transferred to the class E 0-8-0s and their place taken by bogie tenders of the pattern exemplified in model-form.
Photo: Railway Museum, Gävle

Britain. Efficient and elegant was the three-cylinder compound locomotive of the Midland Railway. It was also the most successful compound design in Britain and formed the most numerous class of British 4-4-0. One of them accomplished a run that has never been equalled by any other 4-4-0 in these islands; in 1928 No. 1054 ran non-stop and on schedule the 399¾ miles from London to Edinburgh.

Based on a system devised by W. M. Smith, the Midland-trained Chief Draughtsman of the North Eastern at Gateshead, the first five compounds were completed at Derby in 1902–1903 to the design of S. W. Johnson. Ten more were built in 1905 by his successor R. M. Deeley and these had all the distinctive features which formed the new hallmark of Derby...smokebox door secured by six dogs and displaying a number at its centre, cab with extended roof and beautifully symmetrical high-sided tender with large serif numerals.

The dimensions of the inside 19in. × 26in. high-pressure cylinder, outside 21in. × 26in. low-pressure cylinders and 7ft coupled wheels were unchanged, but the total heating-surface was reduced from 1,598 sq. ft to 1,458 sq. ft and the grate-area and boiler-pressure increased to 28⅝ sq. ft and 220lb./in.² respectively. The tender had a capacity of 3,500 gallons of water and 7 tons of coal. The weight of engine and tender in working order was 105 tons 14½cwt.

Altogether 45 compounds were constructed by the Midland. The LMS built the balance of 195, all of which had 6ft 9in. coupled wheels.

Although they have been modelled extensively on a commercial basis by more than one manufacturer in more than one gauge, super-detail scale-models of Midland compounds are rare. The example illustrated is a working model, with all the loveliness of the prototype. It is a 1 1/16 in. to 1ft, 5in. gauge replica of No. 1012 (originally No. 1007) of 1905 and is owned by R. P. Cole of Aldbury, Herts. It was made by J. F. Adams of Parkstone, Dorset, who also carried out the lining and lettering, the painting being the work of his wife. The boiler is made entirely of copper, with all joints and stays silver soldered, and fitted with 25 ⅜in. tubes. The twin safety-valves are the correct Ramsbottom type. Construction of the model took about 1,500 hours.
Photo: R. P. Cole

PLATE V

Britain. J. D. Lewin of Leicester made this superb working model of class 8B Great Central Railway Atlantic No. 361 for Humphrey Platts of Grantham. Research and drawings were taken in hand in 1968 and it was completed in the latter part of 1972.

It is built to a scale of $1\frac{1}{16}$ in. to 1ft, 5in. gauge. The cylinders are $1\frac{7}{8}$ in. $\times$ $2\frac{1}{4}$ in. and the coupled wheels $7\frac{5}{16}$ in. The equipment includes a four-element superheater. Under test it has run non-stop for one hour and has shown that it can haul 12 adults with ease.

The full-size locomotive was designed by J. G. Robinson, Chief Mechanical Engineer of the Great Central, and built at the company's Gorton works in 1906. The pioneer of the class had appeared three years earlier. The two cylinders were $19\frac{1}{2}$ in. $\times$ 26in., the coupled wheels 6ft 9in. and the boiler-pressure 180lb./in.² Heating-surface totalled 1,911 sq. ft and the grate-area 26 sq. ft. In working order engine and tender weighed $118\frac{3}{4}$ tons, the tender holding 4,000 gallons of water and 6 tons of coal. With their curvaceous bodies and opulent livery, the Great Central Atlantics were among the loveliest engines Robinson ever put on the road. They were dubbed *Jersey Lilies*, inspired by the charms of Lily Langtry, a reigning beauty of the period.
Photo: Studio Colophon Ltd

PLATE VI

Switzerland. When the Simplon tunnel was nearing completion, some doubts were expressed about the use of steam-traction through its great length of 12 miles 537 yards. As a result, the Brown Boveri Co. of Baden put forward a scheme for its electrification, at the same time offering two electric-locomotives then in hand for the Italian State Railways. The idea was adopted and the electrification of the tunnel section between Brigue and Iselle with three-phase a/c 16⅔ cycles was carried out. One of the locomotives in model-form is illustrated. It is the Swiss Transport Museum $\frac{1}{10}$th scale replica of Swiss Federal Railways 900 hp 1-C-1 No. 365, as built in 1906 by Brown Boveri in co-operation with the Swiss Locomotive Works. The model was made in 1913–1914 by Brown Boveri.

The full-size prototype had three pairs of driving-wheels actuated directly by two motors, the middle pair through a yoke and the outer pairs by conventional coupling-rods. The motors were constructed for two speeds, 34 and 68 kmph, the drawbar-pull at the lesser being 6 tons and at the greater 3½ tons. The leading and trailing trucks were of the Bissel type. Mounted rather far apart so as to bridge 'dead' sections of overhead line at points and crossings, the two collectors, each provided with sliding contacts insulated from each other, collected current from two parallel overhead conductor-wires. Total weight of the locomotive was 62 tons, with 42 tons available for adhesion.
Photo: Swiss Transport Museum, Lucerne

Britain. The North British Atlantic was a rather majestic-looking locomotive, combining Great Central and North Eastern features respectively in the shape of its running-plate and cab. The fine model reproduced of *Waverley*, the ninth of the class, was made by C. Rae of Glasgow to a scale of 1in. to 1ft and acquired by the Royal Scottish Museum in 1927. It wears the LNER apple-green livery and the number allotted by that company; in North British days it was No. 876.

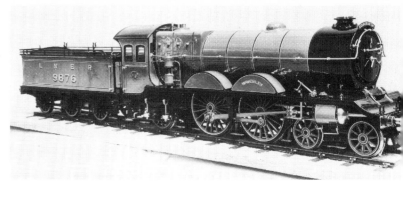

Twenty-two Atlantics were built, Nos. 868–881 by the North British Locomotive Co. in 1906, Nos. 901–906 by Robert Stephenson & Co. in 1911 and Nos. 509–510 by the first-named in 1920. All bore names, these being associated with the areas they traversed on the Edinburgh–Aberdeen and Edinburgh–Carlisle main lines. Originally the coupled wheels were 6ft 9in. and the two cylinders 20in. × 28in. The 15ft boiler-barrel and 9ft Belpaire firebox provided a total heating-surface of 2,256$\frac{1}{5}$ sq. ft, with 28$\frac{1}{2}$ sq. ft of grate-area. Three safety-valves were mounted in triangular layout on the firebox, the working-pressure being 200lb./in.[2]. With a full load of 4,240 gallons of water and 7 tons of coal the engine and tender weighed 119$\frac{1}{5}$ tons. *Waverley* remained in service until 1937.
Photo: Royal Scottish Museum, Edinburgh

U.S.A. This well-proportioned model 2-6-0 owes its existence to the construction of the Panama Canal early in the present century. It was made by Bassett-Lowke Ltd, probably to a scale of $\frac{3}{4}$in. to 1ft, for the Isthmian Canal Commission, but the date it was completed is not known. According to Andrew Merrilees of Toronto, its prototype was one of 20 engines built in 1906 by the American Locomotive Co. to the unusual track-gauge of 5ft. The works Nos. were 39122–39141 and the road Nos. 601–620. Cylinders were 20in. × 26in., coupled wheels were 5ft 3in. diameter, the boiler-pressure being 180lb. and the tractive effort 25,257lb. Weight of the locomotive and tender was nearly 105 tons, the latter carrying 3,300 gallons of water and 6 tons of coal.

After the canal had been finished all the engines were disposed of in 1917. Twelve were sold to the Grand Trunk Railway, renumbered 1,100–1,111 and converted to standard gauge for operation in Michigan. There they remained, even after their new owner in 1923, the Canadian National, took over the Grand Trunk and designated it Grand Trunk Western. On the latter they were class E92 and renumbered 890–901. Two were sold in 1934 to the Detroit, Caro & Sandusky Railway, by which time the others had been scrapped. The remaining eight were transferred to the Alaska Railroad which, like the canal and the railway (better known as the Panama Railroad), is owned by the United States Government. They too had to be converted to 4ft 8$\frac{1}{2}$in. gauge.
Photo: Bassett-Lowke Ltd

Britain. This compact little 2-6-2T is a 16mm. to 1ft working-replica of the locomotive *Russell* as originally built for the erstwhile North Wales Narrow Gauge Railways. Running on 1$\frac{1}{4}$in. gauge track, it was completed in 1962 by Allan Pratt of Birmingham, after some 830 hours had been spent upon its construction. The model is steam-operated, its boiler embodying a central flue, with cross water-tubes, and working at a pressure of 60lb./in.[2]. Spirit is accommodated in one side-tank and water in the other. Water is fed into the boiler by an axle-driven pump or hand-pump. There is a lubricator beneath the front footplate. With its correct NWNGR livery of Midland crimson lake, lined-out black and yellow, setting off its polished brass dome, the model presents a most attractive appearance.

The 1ft 11½in. gauge prototype was built in 1906 by the Hunslet Engine Co. of Leeds (maker's No. 901), being an enlargement of an earlier design for the 2ft 6in. gauge Sierra Leone Government Railway. The cylinders were 10¾in. × 15in. and the coupled wheels 2ft 4in. The boiler had a diameter of 3ft 1½in., length of 8ft 1½in. and worked at 160lb./in.². The grate-area was 6¼ sq. ft and the total heating surface 381 sq. ft. In working order the weight was 19 tons 6 cwt. *Russell* became Welsh Highland Railway stock in 1922. Soon afterwards its chimney, dome and cab were cut down so that it might work through the Moelwyn tunnel. The changes were aesthetically disastrous, and Welsh narrow-gauge historian J. I. C. Boyd was provoked to observe that the changes had turned *Russell* into 'one of the most loutish locomotives to be seen on the two-foot gauge'.
Photo: Dr A. J. Pearce

Germany. When the Deutsche Reichsbahn was formed in 1920 by the fusion of seven State systems, one of the comparatively few locomotive-types to survive and continue to multiply was the Prussian class P8 two-cylinder 4-6-0. The DR designation of these engines was class 38^{10-40}. Over the years 1906–1923 more than 3,000 were constructed by five of the leading German locomotive-builders, Borsig, Schwartzkopff, Vulkan, Henschel and Maschinenbaugesellschaft. Large numbers were handed over to the Allies at the end of World War I.

They were efficient but rather too light, their weight with tender being a little over 119 tons in working order, the engine accounting for 72½ tons. The cylinders were 22⅝in. × 24⅘in., the coupled wheels 5ft 8 9/10in. and the working-pressure 176lb./in.², giving a tractive power of 24,880lb. Total heating-surface was 1,620 sq. ft and grate-area 30 sq. ft. In the museum at Nürnberg there is an excellent model of No. 38.1000, made to a scale of 1/10th.
Photo: Verkehrsmuseum, Nürnberg

Britain. Although models of the Midland Railway 4-4-0 No. 999 were produced on a commercial basis under the auspices of Bassett-Lowke Ltd before World War I, very few super-detail examples have been made. The finest extant is probably the 5in. gauge, $1\frac{1}{16}$in. to 1ft working scale-model illustrated. It took Peter Dupen from 1951 to 1963 to build. This beautiful model, which typifies the simplicity of British steam-locomotive design at its best, lacks only one feature of its prototype. The distinctive tender fire-iron supports have been omitted to avoid risk of injury to the wrists and forearms of the person driving, who sits on a flat wagon immediately behind the tender. In other respects the equipment is complete and includes working Ramsbottom safety-valves, Deeley cross-drive valve-gear (a form of Walschaerts gear), outside admission piston-valves, steam-sanding, full working steam and vacuum-brakes and water pick-up gear on the tender. At the *Model Engineer* Exhibition of 1964 the locomotive was awarded a silver medal and the Crebbin Memorial Trophy. Six years later, under public test, it performed a non-stop run of 30 minutes, hauling a load of ten adult passengers 8,300 yards at $9\frac{2}{5}$ mph and consuming two gallons of water and $2\frac{7}{10}$lb. of coal in the process.

Its principal dimensions compared with those of the full-size locomotive are set out below:

	Model	*Prototype* (*as built*)
Cylinders	$1\frac{1}{8}$in. $\times$ $2\frac{1}{8}$in.	19in. $\times$ 26in.
Coupled wheels	$6\frac{15}{16}$in.	6ft $6\frac{1}{2}$in.
Heating surface	465 sq. in.	$1,557\frac{2}{5}$ sq. ft.
Superheater surface	36 sq. in.	
Grate area	$22\frac{2}{5}$ sq. in.	$28\frac{2}{5}$ sq. ft
Working pressure	100lb./in.^{2}	220lb./in.^{2}
Tractive effort	58lb.	16,165lb.
Operational weight:		
Locomotive	132lb.	$58\frac{1}{2}$ tons
Tender	80lb.	$45\frac{9}{10}$ tons
Total	212lb.	$104\frac{2}{5}$ tons

When the prototype, which was built in 1907, had proved its worth, nine further engines, Nos. 990–998, were constructed in 1909. They were stationed at Carlisle for working express passenger-trains over the heavily graded main line to Leeds. By January 1914 all ten had been fitted with superheaters.

Photo: E. Roddis

Sweden. Swedish State Railways class E 0-8-0 locomotives numbered 130. They were constructed for the Norrlands lines during 1907–1920 and although primarily designed for freight service were also used on passenger trains. Their distinctive characteristics have been reproduced in this $\frac{1}{10}$th scale-model of No. 1187, made in the SJ Örebro workshops in 1916. The prototype had been built by Nydqvist & Holm three years previously. These engines have a tractive effort of 19,800lb. Their cylinders are 19$\frac{3}{8}$in. × 24$\frac{1}{4}$in. and coupled wheels 4ft 6$\frac{3}{4}$in., the weight in working order being 82$\frac{7}{10}$ tons. All have been preserved and the first of the class, No. 900, is stored in the Railway Museum at Gävle.
Photo: Railway Museum, Gävle

Egypt. Staff of the Egyptian State Railways workshops at Cairo made this fine $\frac{1}{8}$th scale, 7$\frac{1}{4}$in. gauge working model of 4-6-0 No. 725 *Abbas Hilmy His Highness the Khedive* in 1908. It was constructed for display at the Franco-British Exhibition of that year. The prototype was built by the North British Locomotive Co. in 1907 to the designs of F. H. Trevithick, Chief Mechanical Engineer of the ESR and grandson of the immortal Richard. He headed locomotive, carriage and wagon affairs at Cairo from 1883 until 1912, which resulted in much standardisation in the English style and the use of an attractive locomotive-livery of reddish brown, lined black and vermilion.

No. 725 had 19in. × 26in. cylinders, with valves actuated by Walschaerts gear. The coupled wheels were 6ft 3in. and the working-pressure 180lb./in.². Heating-surface of the firebox was 172 sq. ft and of the tubes 2,149 sq. ft. The engine weighed 68$\frac{3}{4}$ tons, with over 51 tons adhesive; the tender held 4,000 gallons of water and 6 tons of coal; and the total weight of the two in working order was 112$\frac{1}{4}$ tons. Its handsome proportions were somewhat marred by the extended smokebox, which was to accommodate feed-water heating apparatus designed to utilise heat thrown up the chimney.
Photo: Science Museum, London

Canada. Because of the heavily industrial character of the area served by the Toronto, Hamilton & Buffalo Railway, switching engines have always predominated in its motive power, of which 0-6-0 No. 41 was once a typical example. This delightful little ¼in. to 1ft scale-model of that locomotive is in the collection of Andrew Merrilees of Toronto. Its equipment includes replicas of the canvas sheets which are drawn across the gangway and down over the back of the cab, during the cold Canadian winter.

The full-size No. 41 was constructed at Montreal Locomotive Works in 1908 with 19in. × 26in. cylinders and 4ft 3in. coupled wheels. It had a working-pressure of 180lb./in.², giving a tractive power of 26,000lb., and was the solitary occupant of class B1 in the company's roster. It was sold to Fraser Co. Ltd of Edmundston, New Brunswick in 1926 and scrapped 20 years later.

Photo: Andrew Merrilees Ltd

Belgium. In his nostalgic *Nos Inoubliables Vapeur*, Phil Dambly divides his comprehensive survey of Belgian steam-locomotive development into 12 eras. The seventh, covering the years 1898–1908, is sub-titled *Régime McIntosh*, which will sound strange to young readers. J. F. McIntosh was in that period Locomotive Superintendent of the Caledonian Railway and a firm believer in boilers of generous dimensions. His *Dunalastair* series of 4-4-0s were so successful that in 1898 the Belgian State Railways ordered five similar to his class 766 engines, even to the bogie tenders and blue livery. They became class 17. Thereafter there grew up a fleet of 4-4-0s, 4-4-2 tanks, 4-6-0s and 0-6-0s of McIntosh lineaments, all built on the Continent for the Belgian State system.

Most numerous were the class 18 4-4-0s, of which 140 were constructed between 1902 and 1905. They had 19in. × 26in. cylinders, 6ft 6in. coupled wheels, a total heating-surface of 1,373 sq. ft and a grate-area of $22\frac{3}{10}$ sq. ft, the working-pressure being 175lb./in.². Final version of the McIntosh 4-4-0 was the class 18 *bis* (later class 20), which is represented by the model illustrated of No. 3902, made to a scale of $\frac{1}{10}$th by engineering pupils at Gentbrugge. Fifteen of these engines were completed in 1908. They differed from the class 18 locomotives in that they were given Flamme-type bogies and six-wheeled tenders. They weighed 56 tons.

Photo: SNCB

Holland. The North Brabant Railway or, to give it its full Dutch title, Noord-Brabantsch-Duitsche Spoorweg Maatschappij, connected Boxtel, in Holland, with Wesel, in Germany, a distance of 62¾ miles. At one time it formed an important international link for mail and freight traffic. It is represented in the Railway Museum in Utrecht by a $\frac{1}{10}$th scale-model of one of its beautiful 4-6-0 express locomotives, No. 31. The model was made during the years 1953–1959 in the museum repair-shop by C. J. Honig.

These engines were built by Beyer Peacock & Co. in 1908 and were the first six-coupled express locomotives in Holland. They carried the maker's Nos. 5134–5139 and were numbered 31–35 in NBDS stock. Their English appearance was remarkably strong. There was a Great Central look about the dome, the four-column Ramsbottom safety-valves and the tender. And the cab, the Westinghouse air-pump and the dark blue livery, with black borders and red lines, recalled the Great Eastern. The inside cylinders were 19in. × 26in., inclined at 1 in 24. The coupled wheels were 6ft 6in. and the boiler-pressure 200lb./in.², which was exceptionally high compared with Dutch practice elsewhere at that time. The grate-area was 28 sq. ft and the heating-surface 1,536 sq. ft. In working order the engine and tender weighed 98 tons. Locomotives Nos. 30–32 were fitted with superheaters in 1917 and the others were similarly dealt with after the line had become part of the Netherlands Railways.
Photo: Railway Museum, Utrecht

Switzerland. Another $\frac{1}{10}$th scale-model of a compound locomotive in the Swiss Transport Museum is this fine reproduction of four-cylinder 4-6-0 No. 938 of the Gotthard Railway. It was made between 1910 and 1914 by Optiker Friedinger of Lucerne. Its prototype was one of a series constructed by J. A. Maffei of Munich in 1908, being a development of the class A3/5 locomotive illustrated on page 68. A notable feature was the use of only two sets of Heusinger valve-gear, which actuated two piston-valves, each of which distributed steam to a pair of cylinders. The latter were arranged with the high-pressure $15\frac{1}{2}$in. $\times$ $25\frac{1}{8}$in. pair between the frames and the low-pressure 25in. $\times$ $25\frac{1}{8}$in. pair outside. All drove the leading 5ft $3\frac{3}{8}$in. coupled wheels.

These engines had a total heating-surface of 2,540 sq. ft and grate-area of 36 sq. ft. Their working-pressure was 220lb./in.² and weight in working order $115\frac{1}{4}$ tons, including the tender, which had a water-capacity of 3,750 gallons and held $4\frac{3}{4}$ tons of coal. After the Gotthard Railway became a part of the Swiss Federal Railways in 1909, Schmidt super-heaters replaced the Clench steam-dryers with which the engines were originally fitted.
Photo: Swiss Transport Museum, Lucerne

Spain. In 1908 the 5ft 6in. gauge Great Southern Railway of Spain took delivery of three large Kitson-Meyer 2-8-8-0 tank engines, Nos. 50–52, built that year by Kitson & Co. of Leeds. The locomotives were constructed in three sections, the 47ft $4\frac{3}{4}$in. main frame, which carried the boiler, being pivoted each end on two smaller frames carrying the cylinders, motion and wheels. The two sets of eight-coupled wheels were 4ft in diameter and the four high-pressure cylinders were $14\frac{3}{4}$in. $\times$ 24in. The boiler, 15ft long and 5ft 6in. in diameter, carried a working-pressure of 180lb./in.² and was fed by two double-acting Worthington pumps. Automatic vacuum-brake was provided. Side and bunker tanks held 2,300 gallons of water and the coal capacity was $2\frac{1}{2}$ tons, the total weight in working order being 101 tons, of which $90\frac{1}{10}$ tons were available for adhesion.

The Science Museum model of No. 50 illustrated is built to a scale of $\frac{1}{48}$th. It is owned by Lt.Col. E. Kitson Clark.
Photo: Science Museum, London

Sweden. The most powerful steam-locomotives of the Swedish State Railways were the five class R 0-10-0s, of which two were built by Motala in 1908 and the remainder by Nydqvist & Holm in the following year. They were designed for the haulage of iron-ore trains on the Abisko-Riksgränsen line, on which they worked until its electrification in 1915, when they were transferred to ordinary freight services elsewhere on the system.

These massive engines were given two $24\frac{1}{5}$in. $\times$ $27\frac{1}{2}$in. cylinders and 4ft $2\frac{1}{10}$in. coupled wheels. Their tractive effort was 40,400lb. and they weighed 130 tons in working order. The three built by Nydqvist & Holm have been preserved for military purposes. SJ workshops at Örebro made the $\frac{1}{10}$th scale-model of No. 978 in 1915.

Another new type which also made its *début* in 1908 was the class Sa 2-6-2 suburban-traffic tank engine. Forty-six were constructed by Falun up to 1916. Their cylinders were $19\frac{3}{8}$in. $\times$ $22\frac{4}{5}$in., coupled wheels 6ft $0\frac{1}{5}$in. and tractive effort 15,620lb., the operational weight being $62\frac{7}{10}$ tons. None is now in service, the whole class having been put into mothballs. The attractive $\frac{1}{10}$th scale-model of No. 1058 is an Örebro production of 1914.

Photos: Railway Museum, Gävle

Algeria. An unusual rejuvenation of a Bourbonnais 0-6-0 is exemplified by this $\frac{1}{10}$th scale-model of No. 214 of the Algerian Eastern Railway, displayed in the Paris Musée des Techniques. The original full-size engine was supplied to the railway company by the Société Alsacienne de Constructions Mécaniques and conversion to 4-6-0 took place in 1909. The two outside $17\frac{7}{10}$in. $\times$ $25\frac{1}{2}$in. cylinders with inside flat valves and 4ft 11in. coupled wheels were retained, but the frame was lengthened and a leading bogie added to take a new Belpaire boiler with a working-pressure of 200lb./in.^{2}. The original diminutive four-wheeled tender, which weighed only $21\frac{1}{5}$ tons in operational order, was also retained.

Much of the exterior of the righthand side of the model, such as the whole of the smokebox, boiler and firebox clothing, the coupled-wheel splashers and parts of the chimney, dome, cylinder and cab side-sheet, are cut away to show internal details. The cab has its full quota of fittings.
Photo: Musée des Techniques CNAM, Paris

South Africa. The first Mallet-type locomotive to operate in South Africa was 2-6-6-0 compound No. 336, built by the American Locomotive Co. for the Natal Government Railways in 1909. It was used for the banking of heavy coal-trains on the main line between Estcourt and Highlands, with such satisfactory results that an order was placed for five more. These, however, arrived after the formation of the South African Railways and were slightly larger and more powerful.

All the leading characteristics of No. 336 have been faithfully reproduced in the model illustrated. It was made by the META consortium in 1951–1952, to a scale of 7mm. to 1ft, and is preserved in the Railway Museum at Johannesburg. No. 336 had 17½in. × 26in. high-pressure and 28in. × 26in. low-pressure cylinders. The coupled wheels were 3ft 9½in., and with a working-pressure of 200lb./in.² the tractive effort was 44,810lb. There was 2,574 sq. ft of heating-surface and the grate-area amounted to 40 sq. ft. The overall length of the engine and tender was 68ft 2⅜in. and the weight in working order 129 tons 8½ cwt, there being 4,000 gallons of water and 8¼ tons of coal in the bogie tender. On South African Railways No. 336 became No. 1601, class MA.
Photo: SAR Publicity & Travel Department

South Africa. The last locomotives to be built for the Central South African Railways, before they became part of the South African Railways in 1910, were ten Pacifics, five of which were saturated and five superheated. They began to go into service in 1910 and respectively became classes 10A and 10B of the SAR. In the Railway Museum at Johannesburg is a well finished 7mm. to 1ft scale-model of one of the superheated engines. It was made in 1951–1952 by the META consortium.

Design of the prototype closely followed that of the CSAR class 10 Pacific of 1904. The coupled wheels of 5ft 2in. diameter were repeated and were still the largest yet used in South Africa. With cylinders 20in. × 28in. and a working-pressure of 180lb./in.² the tractive effort was 24,390lb. Total heating-surface amounted to 1,588 sq. ft, the Schmidt superheater-area to 384 sq. ft and the grate-area to 35 sq. ft. The working-order weight was 123¼ tons, which included 1,000 gallons of water and 10 tons of coal in the bogie tender.
Photo: SAR Publicity & Travel Department

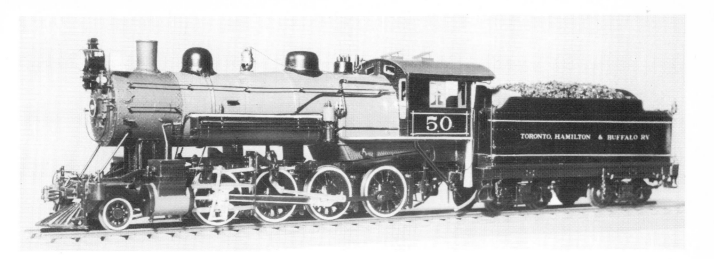

Canada. Another attractive ¼in. to 1ft scale-model in the collection of Andrew Merrilees is this replica of class G 2-8-0 No. 50 of the Toronto, Hamilton & Buffalo Railway, depicting it in the form in which it was originally built. The prototype was the first of a group of seven, Nos. 50–56 and later Nos. 101–107, constructed between 1910 and 1912 by the Montreal Locomotive Works. The cylinders were 23in. × 28in., the coupled wheels 4ft 7in. and the boiler-pressure 200lb./in.², producing a tractive effort of 45,780lb. Weight was a little over 91 tons.

About 1912 the headlight of No. 50 was lowered to the centre of the boilerhead and five years later the engine was equipped with piston-valves and superheater. Early in 1918, when it had become No. 70, it was wrecked in a collision with a stationary freight train. After rebuilding, it was again renumbered, becoming No. 101, and the remainder of the class were renumbered in the same group. It was scrapped in 1945. One of its sister engines, No. 103, was placed in Gage Park, Hamilton in 1956 and is now preserved there.
Photo: Andrew Merrilees Ltd

Britain. The *George the Fifth* class superheated 4-4-0s, of which 90 were constructed between 1910 and 1915, were among the best known locomotives of the London & North Western Railway. Commercial models of this class were turned out in thousands before World War I in clockwork, electric and steam versions for the smaller gauges. In the Great Hall at old Euston station it was represented by a coin-in-the-slot ¾in. to 1ft scale-model of No. 5000 *Coronation*, which had been built at Crewe in 1911 and was the 5000th locomotive to be completed there. The model was, it is believed, made there in the same year; it will be seen that the smokebox is partly cut away to show the interior. After the formation of the London Midland & Scottish Railway in 1923 it was repainted in the first passenger-engine livery of that company, Midland crimson lake, lined black and yellow, with gilt LMS on the cab-sides and the new number on the tender-sides. It is now in the Museum of British Transport.

Full-size *Coronation* had 20½in. × 26in. cylinders, 6ft 9in. coupled wheels and a working-pressure of 175lb./in.². The total heating-surface was 1,849¾ sq. ft, including

$302\frac{1}{2}$ sq. ft of the Schmidt superheater, and the grate-area was $22\frac{2}{5}$ sq. ft. The tender was fitted with water pick-up gear and held 3,000 gallons of water and 7 tons of coal. In working order the engine and tender weighed $99\frac{1}{10}$ tons. It was taken out of service in 1940 and broken up two years later.

Photo: London Midland & Scottish Railway

France. The Paris Musée des Techniques displays a fine $\frac{1}{10}$th scale-model of one of the impressive 2-8-2 superheated tank engines of the Eastern Railway of France, of which 102 were constructed over the years 1911–1917. The model is in the livery of the French Railways (SNCF), on which the series were class 141-TB, renumbered between 401 and 512; it is not provided with the usual clothing to the smokebox, boiler and firebox.

These locomotives had 5ft $2\frac{1}{5}$in. coupled wheels and cylinders $21\frac{3}{5}$in. × 26in. with piston-valves actuated by Walschaerts gear. The boiler had a total heating-surface of $1,387\frac{1}{2}$ sq. ft, with a further $398\frac{1}{5}$ sq. ft provided by the Schmidt superheater, and a grate-area of $25\frac{1}{5}$ sq. ft. Weight in working order was $87\frac{1}{2}$ tons and the maximum service speed 90 kmph.

Photo: Musée des Techniques CNAM, Paris

Austria. Karl Gölsdorf, Chief of the Locomotive, Carriage and Wagon section of the Austrian Railway Ministry from 1891 until 1916, was a locomotive-designer of the front rank. Technically accomplished, inventive, adventurous and not enamoured of excessive standardisation, he was to the Austrian State Railways what Gresley was to the LNER in Britain. His best-known design is represented in the Austrian Railway Museum by this fine, fully detailed scale-model of 2-6-4 No. 310.53, the first of which class of superheated express locomotives appeared in 1911. In that year seven such engines each were constructed at the four locomotive works Floridsdorf, Wiener Neustadt, First Bohemian and Steg. They were assigned to the haulage of passenger trains between Vienna, Cracow and Lemberg, and Vienna and Linz, with maximum speeds of 100 kmph.

These distinctive locomotives, which had a look of the greyhound about them, were four-cylinder compounds. Both the inside high-pressure $15\frac{1}{2}$in. $\times$ $28\frac{1}{2}$in. and outside low-pressure 26in. $\times$ $28\frac{1}{2}$in. cylinders drove the centre pair of 7ft 1in. coupled wheels. The leading pair of carrying-wheels were arranged in the form of a Krauss-Helmholtz truck and the four trailing wheels in a bogie of the Bissel type. The boiler had parallel back and front rings and a long tapered middle ring, with outside diameters of 5ft $10\frac{3}{4}$in. and 5ft $5\frac{3}{4}$in. at back and front respectively. Evaporative heating-surface was 2,290 sq. ft and the Schmidt superheater had a heating-surface of 465 sq. ft, the grate-area being $49\frac{3}{4}$ sq. ft. The working-pressure was 213lb./in.² By 1916 there was a fleet of 90 and they worked Austrian expresses until well after World War I. **Right** footplate of locomotive No. 310.53.

The model is a fine example of the skill of Josef Stögermayr. Made to $\frac{1}{30}$th scale, it took 10,000 hours of his time during 1922–1924.

Photos: Austrian Railway Museum, Vienna

Italy. Models of two classes of Pacific express locomotives of the Italian State Railways are to be seen in the Museo Nazionale della Scienza e della Tecnica Leonardo da Vinci in Milan. Both have been made to $\frac{1}{20}$th scale. The model of the earlier prototype, the class 690, is of especial interest because it was constructed entirely of wood by the architect Pasini of Milan. The other model, of the class 691 prototype, is partly sectionalised; it will be seen that the running-plate and parts of the cab, firebox and boiler-casing are cut away to reveal the internal layout.

There were 33 class 690 locomotives, the first being built by Breda of Milan. They were constructed over the years 1911–1914, chiefly for the haulage of expresses between Milan and Bologna. They were four-cylinder simple engines, the cylinders being $17\frac{3}{4}$in. $\times$ $26\frac{3}{4}$in., the coupled wheels 6ft $7\frac{7}{8}$in. and the boiler-pressure 171lb./in.² Total heating-surface was $2,262\frac{1}{2}$ sq. ft, the superheater-surface $721\frac{1}{2}$ sq. ft and the grate-area $37\frac{3}{5}$ sq. ft. The double-bogie tender held 8 tons of coal and 4,400 gallons of water and the total weight of the engine and tender in working order was $134\frac{3}{4}$ tons.

The class 691 engines were designed to meet the demand for better steaming capacity and a more generous firebox. This was achieved with a boiler 2ft longer, a boiler-pressure of 199lb./in.², a total heating-surface of 2,551 sq. ft and a grate-area of $46\frac{1}{5}$ sq. ft. In almost all other respects their dimensions were the same as those of the class 690 engines, although they were given tenders of 45 per cent greater capacity. Florence works of the Italian State Railways turned out the first class 691 locomotive in 1928.

Photos: Museo Nazionale della Scienza e della Tecnica Leonardo da Vinci, Milan

Australia. Very few good models of Australian steam locomotives have been made. One of the best is to be seen in this country, in the Transport Museum in Glasgow. It is a splendid ⅛th. scale replica of 2-8-0 class T (later class D 50) locomotive No. 1258 (No. 5231 in 1924) of the New South Wales Government Railways. The name of its maker is not known.

Its prototype belonged to a class that eventually consisted of 280 engines, the strongest group numerically of any on this system. The first were constructed in 1896 by Beyer Peacock & Co., as saturated locomotives, with 4ft 3in. coupled wheels, 21in. × 26in. cylinders, and a 160lb./in.² boiler-pressure, giving a tractive effort of 28,000lb. Later engines, some of which were superheated, had 22in.- diameter cylinders, thus raising the tractive effort to 33,600lb. No. 1258

was one of them, being built by the North British Locomotive Co. in 1914. Steam distribution was effected by Allan straight-link valve-gear, and the second and third pairs of coupled wheels were flangeless. The total heating-surface was 2,117 sq. ft, which included 364 sq. ft of the superheater, and the grate-area was 28¾ sq. ft. Engine and tender measured 60ft 3¾in. over buffers and together weighed 112 tons 13 cwt in working order; the capacity of the tender was 3,650 gallons of water and 9½ tons of coal.

The class was employed on all lines of the system, taking steep grades and sharp curves in their stride. Fourteen of these grand old engines, with their distinctive porthole cabs, are still in service in the Port Waratah area on coal-traffic haulage and shunting duties.
Photo: Museum of Transport, Glasgow

PLATE VII

France. In 1916 British locomotive-builders undertook the construction of 90 Pacific express passenger and 150 Consolidation freight engines for the French State Railways. The design of these locomotives adhered strictly to French practice. The Pacifics were four-cylinder de Glehn-du Bousquet superheated compounds and the freight engines were two-cylinder simples.

North British Locomotive Co. built some of the Pacifics, one of which, No. 231.650, is represented by this handsome model. This was made to $\frac{1}{10}$th scale, but its maker is not known. It is to be seen in the Glasgow Transport Museum.

The full-size locomotive had outside $16\frac{1}{8}$in. × $25\frac{3}{8}$in. high-pressure cylinders driving the intermediate pair of 6ft $4\frac{3}{10}$in. coupled wheels and inside $25\frac{1}{8}$in. × $25\frac{3}{8}$in. low-pressure cylinders actuating the leading pair. Steam-distribution was by means of piston-valves for the outside cylinders and flat balance slide-valves for those inside, with independently controlled Walschaerts gear for both. The engine could therefore be worked as a four-cylinder simple when maximum tractive effort was needed.

A boiler of generous proportions, 5ft $6\frac{1}{8}$in. in diameter at the front ring, was provided. It had a total of $2,281\frac{3}{8}$ sq. ft of evaporative heating-surface, with a 24-element Schmidt superheater creating $683\frac{1}{2}$ sq. ft of heating-surface, and a rocking grate having an area of 46 sq. ft. The working-pressure was $227\frac{1}{2}$lb./in.^{2} and the tractive effort 20,760lb. The tender was carried on two four-wheeled bogies with outside bearings and compensated springs; with its full load of $5\frac{4}{5}$ tons of coal and 4,840 gallons of water it weighed nearly $51\frac{7}{10}$ tons. Operational weight of engine and tender was $146\frac{7}{10}$ tons.

Photo: Museum of Transport, Glasgow

PLATE VIII

Sweden. The 4-6-0 for heavy express passenger-traffic first appeared on the Swedish State Railways in 1909, built by Motala. The example portrayed by the model in the Swedish Railways Museum is No. 1085 of 1911 by the same builder.

These engines, designated class B, had 5ft 6in. coupled wheels, 23¼in. × 24⅜in. cylinders and a working-pressure of 170lb./in.². The heating-surface was made up of 1,682 sq. ft by the tubes and 137 sq. ft by the firebox, with an extra 481 sq. ft by the superheater. The grate-area was 28 sq. ft. The bogie tender had a capacity of 4,000 gallons of water and 6 tons of coal, the total operational weight of the locomotive and tender being 116½ tons. The $\frac{1}{10}$th scale-model was made in the SJ Örebro workshops in 1913.
Photo: Swedish Railway Museum, Gävle

India. Workmen in the Perambur workshops of the Madras & Southern Mahratta Railway made this ⅛th scale-model of 5ft 6in. gauge express passenger 4-6-0 No. 777 between 1920–1922. The railway presented it to the Science Museum.

The prototype was one of four built by Kitson & Co. in 1912, having two cylinders 20in. × 26in. with Howe's link-motion and 6ft 2in. coupled wheels. The tractive effort at 90 per cent of the 180lb./in.² working-pressure was 22,767lb.

The boiler, 5ft in diameter and 15⅜ft in length, had a heating-surface of 1,617 sq. ft, supplemented by the 158 sq. ft of the Belpaire firebox. The grate-area was 32 sq. ft. Operational weight of the engine and tender, both equipped with vacuum-brake, was just under 113 tons. The tender capacity was 4,000 gallons of water and 7½ tons of coal.
Photo: Science Museum, London

Thailand. Twelve metre-gauge 4-6-0 locomotives were built for the Royal State Railways of Siam, now known as the State Railway of Thailand, by the North British Locomotive Co. in 1912. A further five were delivered three years later. The two batches were identical and were designated class E. They had $14\frac{1}{2}$in. × 22in. cylinders with Walschaerts gear, 4ft coupled wheels, a working-pressure of 180lb./in.[2] and a total heating-surface of 915 sq. ft. In working order locomotive and tender weighed 58 tons and the tractive effort was 13,009lb.

A well finished $\frac{1}{10}$th scale-model of No. 156 of 1912 was made in the central workshops of the railway at Makkasan in 1938. It depicts the prototype after oil-firing equipment and smoke-deflector plates had been fitted.
Photo: State Railway of Thailand

France. Twenty four-cylinder de Glehn compound Pacifics were constructed by the Société Alsacienne of Belfort for the Northern Railway of France (Chemin de fer du Nord) in 1912. They were Nos. 3.1151–3.1170, the last one of which is represented in the Musée des Techniques by this excellent model. It was made by Duhamel to $\frac{1}{10}$th scale. These engines were given $16\frac{3}{8}$in. × $26\frac{3}{8}$in. high-pressure and $23\frac{5}{8}$in. × $26\frac{3}{8}$in. low-pressure cylinders, each with its own valve-gear. The coupled wheels were 6ft $8\frac{1}{2}$in. and the boiler-pressure 227lb./in.[2]. Heating-surface was made up of 1,623 sq. ft by the tubes, 183 sq. ft by the firebox and 521 sq. ft by the Schmidt-Nord superheater. The grate-area was $33\frac{9}{10}$ sq. ft. In working order the weight was 85 tons, of which $49\frac{3}{4}$ tons were adhesive.

The model is of particular interest because it has attached to it a bogie tender of the type introduced by the Nord in 1928–1931 for its Pacific locomotives assigned to fast non-stop runs Paris–Calais, Paris–Brussels and Paris–Lille. The purpose of the new tender was to enable sufficient coal and water to be carried so that service-stops could be eliminated. Its capacity was 9 tons of coal and 7,709 gallons of water. It will be noticed that the tender has a rounded top similar to that provided the Great Eastern 4-4-0 on page 62. The coal was carried in a self-trimming, elliptical hopper-shaped bunker at the leading end. The bogies had cast-steel frames and the 4ft $1\frac{1}{8}$in. wheels ran in Isothermos axleboxes. At high speeds the running was said to be remarkably steady.
Photo: Musée des Techniques CNAM, Paris

Britain. When the thriving and bustling little London, Tilbury & Southend Railway decided upon a new design of express passenger-locomotive in 1912, a 1in. scale-model of it was made in the company's Plaistow works for testing on layouts of the sharpest curves and crossovers. Then the model was completed in all external details: it was painted the elaborate LT&S livery by the paint-shop foreman, given No. 94 and named *Arthur Lewis Stride* after the chairman. Meanwhile, the construction of the eight most handsome locomotives of which it was the harbinger was taken in hand by Beyer Peacock & Co. They were the first Baltic or 4-6-4 tank engines to run in Great Britain and were allotted the Nos. 87–94. They were given 20in. × 26in. cylinders, 6ft 3in. coupled wheels, a 5ft diameter boiler having a working-pressure of 160lb./in.² and a Schmidt superheater. The grate-area was 25sq. ft and the total heating-surface 1,446 sq. ft.

By the time they were nearing completion their owner had been acquired by the Midland Railway and they left the paint shop in the crimson lake livery of that company, which numbered them 2100–2107. The model, which is now in the Science Museum, London, is not only unusual because it preceded its prototype, but unique in that it was the only locomotive built at Plaistow works.

Photo: Crown Copyright, Science Museum, London

Hong Kong. Opened in 1910, the British section of the 4ft 8½in. gauge Kowloon–Canton Railway runs from Kowloon, opposite Hong Kong, to Lo Wu, on the Chinese border, a distance of 22 miles. Occasionally one has had glimpses of the line on television during recent years when some unfortunate Briton, incarcerated for inscrutable Chinese reasons, has at last been released to rejoin his compatriots. In the early life of the railway almost all the traffic was handled by 2-6-4 and 4-6-4 tank engines and the $\frac{1}{12}$th scale-model reproduced depicts No. 3, a 2-6-4 tank built by Kitson & Co. in 1912. It was presented to the Science Museum by Brig.Gen. C. C. Wrigley.

The full-size engine had 19in. × 26in. cylinders and 5ft 1½in. coupled wheels, to which Westinghouse brakes were fitted. The working-pressure was 180lb./in.², at 85 per cent of which the tractive effort amounted to 23,350lb. The boiler, 5ft 4in. in diameter and 11ft 6in. long, had a heating-surface of 1,623 sq. ft. The Belpaire firebox contributed a further 187 sq. ft of heating-surface and 32 sq. ft of grate-area. Tank capacity was 1,900 gallons of water and the bunker held 3½ tons of coal, making the total weight in working order 90$\frac{7}{10}$ tons.

Now that more cordial relations are being developed with the Chinese one can perhaps look forward to the resumption of through express services to and from Canton, a facility of happier days in the past.
Photo: Science Museum, London

Holland. *Zeppelins*, the Dutch nicknamed them, because of their conical smokebox doors, bar frames, high-pitched boilers and windcutter cabs. And despite their English livery of yellow ochre and their brass domes, the rakish form of the Netherlands Central four-cylinder 4-6-0s stamped them as products of J. A. Maffei of Munich. Their resemblance to the standard Maffei 4-6-0 engines then at work on the Bavarian Railways was quite marked. The $\frac{1}{13}$th scale-model of No. 78 in the Railway Museum in Utrecht, made in 1917–1920 by H. A. Dreisen of The Hague, fully portrays the characteristics of the class.

Two, Nos. 71 and 72, were built in 1910 and two more, Nos. 73 and 74, followed in 1911. They demonstrated that they could cope with 28-car passenger trains of 700 tons and four more, Nos. 75–78, were completed in 1913–1914. These latter engines differed from their predecessors in that they were equipped with Schmidt superheaters, drop-grates and a modified front to the cab to eradicate troublesome light reflections. The design of the tender was also altered; the rear bogie was replaced by two rigid axles.

The four cylinders of the class were 15¾in. × 25¼in., the coupled wheels being 6ft 3in. and the boiler-pressure 175lb./in.². The liberal grate-area of 37 sq. ft prevented any shortage of steam. Those engines fitted with Schmidt superheaters had a total heating-surface of 2,226½ sq. ft. The tender held 4,400 gallons of water and 5 tons of coal. In working order the locomotive and tender weighed 120 tons.
Photo: Railway Museum, Utrecht

U.S.A. Severn-Lamb Ltd built this ½in. to 1ft scale-model of Pennsylvania Railroad class K4S express passenger 4-6-2 No. 1737 for the Smithsonian Institution. Its prototype, constructed in the railway company's workshops, appeared in mid-1914. These engines had coned Belpaire fireboxes, the heating-surface of which was 288⅗ sq. ft, with a grate-area of 70 sq. ft. The 237 boiler tubes added a further 3,746⅘ sq. ft of evaporative heating-surface, the Schmidt superheater having a heating-surface of 1,153 $\frac{9}{10}$ sq. ft. The boiler-pressure was 205lb./in.², at 80 per cent of which, with the 27in. × 28in. cylinders and 6ft 8in. coupled wheels, a tractive effort of 41,845lb. was produced. Operational weight of the engine and double-bogie tender was 234 tons, the capacity of the latter being 7,000 gallons of water and 12½ tons of coal.

Between 1914 and 1927 more than 400 of them were built. It was one of the most successful passenger-locomotive designs in the United States.

Photo: Smithsonian Institution, Washington

Sweden. The class F 4-6-2 express locomotives of the Swedish State Railways, the first of which, No. 1200, was completed by Nydqvist & Holm in 1914, were superheated four-cylinder compounds. The high-pressure $16\frac{1}{2}$in. × $25\frac{9}{10}$in. cylinders were placed between the frames and the $24\frac{4}{5}$in. × $25\frac{9}{10}$in. low-pressure cylinders outside. All were inclined at 1 in 9.15. Coupled wheels were 6ft 2in. and an almost unique innovation for the times was the employment of ball-bearings for the bogie and trailing axles. The axle-journals of the tender bogies were equipped likewise. The boiler had a diameter of 5ft 7in. and length of 17ft $4\frac{3}{4}$in. between tube-plates; its working-pressure was 185lb./in.². The total heating-surface, including the superheater-tubes, was 2,770 sq. ft and the grate-area was $38\frac{4}{5}$ sq. ft.

A body of semi-circular sections gave the double-bogie tender an unusual shape. It had a water-capacity of 5,466 gallons and held 6 tons 8 cwt of coal. The weight of the locomotive and tender in working order was $142\frac{3}{4}$ tons. The Swedish Railway Museum model of No. 1201 illustrated was built to $\frac{1}{10}$th scale by the SJ Örebro workshops in 1923.

Photo: Swedish Railway Museum Gävle

China. At the Panama Pacific International Exhibition held in San Francisco in 1915, the American Locomotive Co. exhibited a model of one of the 2-8-8-2 Mallet compound locomotives it had recently built for the Pekin–Kalgan Railway in northern China. Electrically operated and constructed to a scale of $\frac{3}{4}$in. to the foot, this unusual model was supplied by Bassett-Lowke Ltd of Northampton (England). After the exhibition it was presented to the Chinese Government.

In working order the prototype of this model weighed over 185 tons with its tender, which carried 6,000 gallons of water and 10 tons of fuel. The high-pressure cylinders were 20in. × 26in. and the low-pressure cylinders, which were at the leading end, 32in. × 26in., both sets being provided with Walschaerts gear controlled by power reverse. The coupled wheels had a diameter of 4ft 2in. The heating-surface of the tubes was 2,353 sq. ft, of the firebox 263 sq. ft and of the superheater-surface 565 sq. ft. The grate-area was 59.6 sq. ft. When working as a compound the tractive power was 56,500lb. and as a simple 67,800lb. These massive engines were employed on the arduous section between Nankow and Kalgan, where the maximum climb is at 1 in 30, with several stretches of 1 in 40 and curves of 600ft radius.

Photo: Bassett-Lowke Ltd

France. Completed in 1972 by Jean Lenoble and painted by Pierre Jardel, this beautiful 7mm. to 1ft, $1\frac{1}{4}$in. gauge scale-model of Paris–Orleans Pacific No. 3588 is a recent addition to the collection of Henri Girod-Eymery. The latter, as well-informed railway modellers are aware, is responsible for the fascinating Museon di Rodo in the little town of Uzès, which lies a short distance north of Nimes and west of Avignon.

The prototype of No. 3588 was one of a batch (Nos. 3551–3589) built in 1912–1914, following 50 (Nos. 3501–3550) which appeared in 1909–1910. They were four-cylinder de Glehn compounds and were designed by the Paris–Orleans Railway in conjunction with the Société Alsacienne de Constructions Mécaniques of Belfort. They had high-pressure cylinders of $16\frac{1}{2}$in. diameter and low-pressure cylinders of $25\frac{1}{10}$in., the common stroke being $25\frac{3}{8}$in. The coupled wheels were 6ft $4\frac{3}{4}$in. and the working-pressure 235lb./in.^{2}. Heating-surface totalled $2,260\frac{4}{5}$ sq. ft and the grate-area was $46\frac{3}{8}$ sq. ft. Operational weight of the locomotive was 91 tons, of which 52 tons were available for adhesion.

On the easily graded lines from Paris to Bordeaux and to Nantes these engines did a good job. One of André Chapelon's notable achievements in later years was to rebuild them and so double their power.

Photo: Henri Girod-Eymery

Britain. Six powerful 4-6-0 express passenger-locomotives to the design of its Locomotive Superintendent, F. G. Smith, were ordered from R&W Hawthorn, Leslie & Co. by the Highland Railway in 1915. They were allotted Nos. 70–75, but after trials with the first two, No. 70 *River Ness* and No. 71 *River Spey*, the Engineer vetoed their use, because of their weight and other objections. In consequence, they and the four yet to be delivered were sold to the Caledonian Railway, which gave them Nos. 938–943 . . . and Smith resigned. These engines had outside cylinders 21in. × 28in. and 6ft coupled wheels. The boiler worked at 170lb./in.^{2} and embodied a Belpaire firebox, Robinson superheater and Ross pop safety-valves. The heating-surface totalled $1,599\frac{3}{5}$ sq. ft, to which the superheater contributed 463 sq. ft and the firebox $139\frac{3}{10}$ sq. ft; the grate-area was $25\frac{3}{10}$ sq. ft. The tenders held 4,000 gallons of water and $6\frac{1}{2}$ tons of coal and the weight in working order of engine and tender was a little more than $121\frac{1}{2}$ tons.

In 1920 the builders commissioned Twining Models Ltd to make three scale-reproductions of these locomotives, as then running on the Caledonian, and one is to be seen in the Museum of Science & Engineering at Newcastle-upon-Tyne. It is of No. 943, the last of the batch, and is correctly fitted with a cast-iron chimney instead of a built-up one with capuchon, with which Nos. 938 and 939 were first equipped. The model is made to a scale of $\frac{3}{4}$in. to 1ft.

Photo: Museum of Science & Engineering, Newcastle-upon-Tyne

Fiji. In Fiji there are three little 2ft gauge railway systems operated for the movement of sugar cane. Over the longest, which extends for 120 miles from Tarvua, *via* Lautoka to Kavonangasau, a regular free passenger-train service is worked under an agreement between the Fijians and the Colonial Sugar Refining Co. The locomotive assigned to this unusual service was (and maybe still is) a diminutive 4-4-0 built in 1915 by Hudswell Clarke (No. 1118), the only passenger-engine on the island. It had $8\frac{1}{2}$in. $\times$ 12in. outside cylinders, 2ft 6in. coupled wheels and a boiler-pressure of 160lb./in.^{2}. The total heating-surface was 276 sq. ft and the grate-area 6 sq. ft. Engine and tender, which held 600 gallons of water and 3 tons of coal, weighed 21 tons 7 cwt in working order.

As the line is partly in the form of a roadside tramway, a rather bright livery was adopted. The basic colour was green, with upper and lower bands on the tender, edges of the locomotive running-board and most of the buffer-beam painted yellow. The rest of the last-named was red and the whole of the cab-roof was white. The tender interior, locomotive running-board, smokebox and chimney were the customary black, the chimney having a copper cap and the dome a polished brass casing. The engine was known as Lautoka No. 18.

The 16mm. scale working model of this locomotive, as running in 1957, was made by Donald Boreham in 1965–1967. It is electrically driven by an ex-Government 27-volt motor, geared 75-1, and is equipped for two-rail or stud operation, the mode being selected by turning the filler-pipe cover on the tender. All wheels are compensated and current is picked up from all wheels, including those of the tender. In 1967 this model won the Chairman's Trophy of the Model Railway Club.
Photo: A. Stapleton-Garner BSc

South Africa. The South African Railways, an amalgamation of the Cape, Central South African and Natal government-owned systems, came into being on 30 May 1910, the day the Union of South Africa was formed. The first Chief Mechanical Engineer was D. A. Hendrie, Locomotive Superintendent of the former Natal Government Railways, who held office until 1922. One of his earliest designs for the new administration was the class 14 4-8-2 locomotive, of which the accompanying 7mm. to 1ft scale-model in the Railway Museum, Johannesburg, was made in 1951–1952 by the META consortium. It demonstrates what well-proportioned engines they were, with their curvaceous chimneys and domes, commodious cabs and symmetrical bogie tenders. Altogether 60 were built, Nos. 1701–1760, by Robert Stephenson & Co. and Beyer Peacock & Co. over the years 1913–1915. The model depicts No. 1721, a Stephenson engine of the latter year.

The class 14s were primarily for use on the Natal system. They had 22in. × 26in. cylinders, 4ft coupled wheels and a boiler-pressure of 190lb./in.², at 75 per cent of which the tractive effort was 37,360lb. The total heating-surface was 2,362 sq. ft, the superheater-area 540 sq. ft and the grate-area 37 sq. ft. Working order weight of the engine and tender was 141 tons 14 cwt, taking into account the 10 tons of coal and 4,250 gallons of water held by the tender.
Photo: SAR Publicity & Travel Department

Sweden. First to work the iron-ore trains over the Kiruna–Riksgransen line of the Swedish State Railways when it had been electrified in 1915 were the class Oa 1C-C1 electric locomotives. The class Ob engines, represented by this model of No. 32–33, which were built by Asea and Falun in 1917, were of the same design. The Oa and Ob locomotives were of 1,600 hp. They had 3ft 7$\frac{3}{10}$in. coupled wheels and weighed 125$\frac{4}{5}$ tons. The first to be built, Oa No. 1–2, is preserved outside the SJ workshops at Lulea. The model was made to $\frac{1}{10}$th scale in 1923 by the SJ workshops at Örebro.
Photo: Railway Museum, Gävle

New Zealand. This impressive model of New Zealand Railways class Wab 4-6-4 tank engine No. 771 was made by Frank Roberts about 1937. Its scale is $\frac{1}{2}$in. to 1ft, gauge 1$\frac{3}{4}$in., and it is powered by an electric motor. The first Wab locomotives appeared in 1917, when two were constructed by the Government workshops at Addington to the designs of H. H. Jackson, NZR Chief Mechanical Engineer. They were similar in appearance to his class Ab 4-6-2 tender engines, the chief working-parts of the two being interchangeable. The outside cylinders were 17in. × 26in., the coupled wheels 4ft 6in. and the working-pressure 200lb./in.², at 80 per cent of which the tractive effort amounted to 22,250lb. The heating-surface was made up of 772 sq. ft by the tubes, 250 sq. ft by the flues of the Robinson superheater and 123 sq. ft by the firebox. The grate-area was 33 sq. ft. As originally built their weight was 70$\frac{7}{10}$ tons, of which 37$\frac{1}{2}$ tons were available for adhesion. The tank capacity was 1,700 gallons of water and the bunker held 3 tons of coal.

Thirty Wab engines were constructed, mainly in NZR workshops, up to 1927 and in their later years most were concentrated at Auckland and Wellington for suburban-train working. Eleven were converted to class Ab between 1947 and 1957. The others had all been withdrawn by 1965, but two have been saved by preservation groups.

Photo: New Zealand Railways Publicity & Advertising Dept.

U.S.A. The American railways, like those in Britain, were taken over by the State during World War I and USRA— United States Railroad Administration—was set up as the operating agency. Twelve different classes of standard locomotives, capable of working successfully on any line, were developed at the request of USRA and the first of them, the light 2-8-2 or Mikado, is represented by this attractive ½in. to 1ft scale-model in the Smithsonian Institution.

Its prototype was built by Baldwin Locomotive Works in 1918 for the Baltimore & Ohio Railroad. It had 26in. × 30in. cylinders, 5ft 3in. coupled wheels and a boiler-pressure of 200lb./in.². Engine and tender weighed 237 tons in working order. USRA designs were straightforward and perhaps a little conservative. They nevertheless influenced American locomotive practice for the best part of a decade.
Photo: Smithsonian Institution, Washington

Hungary. In the years immediately after World War I the most numerous express passenger-locomotives at work on the Hungarian State Railways were the 4-6-0s of series 328. The first 58 (001–058) were built at Budapest in 1919 and Henschel & Son supplied 100 more. They were followed by others from Budapest. They were massive machines and their rather complex external characteristics have been most skilfully reproduced in this $\frac{1}{10}$th working scale-model of one of the class made by Dr Alex Varga, Chief Councillor of the Hungarian State Railways. Construction started in 1932 and took nine years to complete. It marked the beginning of his fine international collection of scale-model express loco-motives.

The prototype series 328 engines had two cylinders $22\frac{2}{8}$in. $\times$ $25\frac{1}{2}$in., coupled wheels 6ft in diameter and a work-ing-pressure of 176lb./in.². The Brotan-type boiler had a total heating-surface of $1598\frac{2}{8}$ sq. ft, supplemented by $486\frac{3}{10}$ sq. ft of the Schmidt superheater, and a grate-area of 35 sq. ft. At 60 per cent of the boiler-pressure the tractive effort was 17,592lb. Weight of engine and tender in working order was $110\frac{2}{5}$ tons, the weight available for adhesion being $42\frac{7}{10}$ tons. *Photo: Dr Alex Varga*

South Africa. First of the numerous Beyer-Garratt locomotives of the South African Railways was class GA 2-6-0+0-6-2 No. 1649 (later No. 2140) which went into service in the early part of 1921, having been built by Beyer Peacock & Co. Although it was small by comparison with later SAR engines of its kind, it possessed a tractive effort of 47,390lb. at 75 per cent of its 180lb./in.² working-pressure and its operational weight was 133 tons 17 cwts. The four cylinders were 18in. × 26in. and the coupled wheels 4ft. The total heating-surface was 2,554½ sq. ft, the superheater-area 526½ sq. ft and the grate-area 51⅔ sq. ft. Water capacity was 4,600 gallons, with space for 9 tons of coal.

The Beyer-Garratt demonstrated its superiority over the Mallet as regards haulage-power and water and coal consumption, and henceforth was the type chosen where the circumstances called for the use of articulated locomotives. No. 1649 therefore has its place in the story of SAR locomotive development. Fortunately it has been preserved in the form of this beautiful replica, complete with all cab-fittings, in the collection of Henri Petiet of Paris. It was originally owned by Beyer Peacock & Co. and was made for them by Twining Models Ltd to a scale of 1in. to 1ft.
Photo: Henri Petiet

102

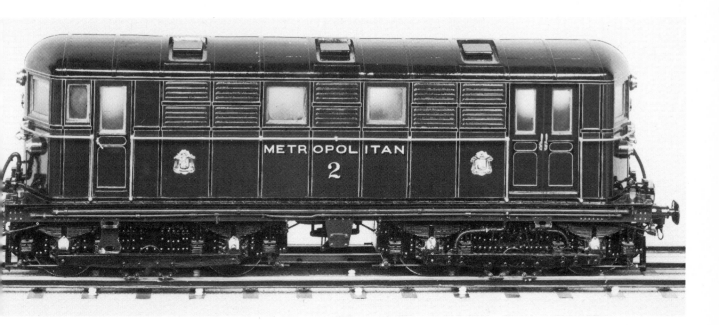

Britain. The last electric-locomotives of the Metropolitan Railway were rebuilds of earlier engines. The work of reconstruction began in 1922 and involved 20 British Thomson-Houston double-bogie products of 1907 and *ante*. When the mechanical parts had been made at the Barrow works of Vickers Ltd and electrical equipment of Metropolitan-Vickers Electrical Co. had been added, comparatively little of the original locomotives remained. With their rich livery of dark crimson lake, lined black and yellow and embellished with transfers of the company's coat of arms, the completed locomotives presented a very pleasing appearance. Two 300 hp self-ventilating motors were mounted on each bogie, which was carried on 3ft 7½in. wheels. The control and other equipment was located along the centre of the body, with ample room each side for inspection and maintenance.

These 1,200 hp locomotives soon established themselves as part of the north-west London suburban scene and demonstrated their worth on 180-ton trains of main-line type stock between Aldgate, Baker Street, Harrow and Rickmansworth. Speeds of up to 65 mph were attained on the long open sections of line. In 1927 they were named after London characters and bronze nameplates replaced the world *Metropolitan*; No. 8, for example, became *Sherlock Holmes* and No. 20 *Sir Christopher Wren*. The drive for scrap-metal in World War II resulted in their removal.

Twining Models Ltd made in 1923 the ¾in. to 1ft reproduction of No. 2, which became *Oliver Cromwell*. Complete in every external detail, it was mounted on short columns so that the wheels cleared the track for about $\frac{1}{32}$ in. Inside the model was fitted a 220 volt electric-motor connected by metal belts to all the wheels. Pressure of a plunger in the base of the showcase containing the model set the wheels in motion.

Photo: Science Museum, London

Britain. Twining Models Ltd also made in 1923 this striking ¾in. to 1ft scale-model of North Eastern Railway 4-6-4 (2-Co-2) electric locomotive No. 13, the wheels of which were similarly actuated. But whereas the prototype of the Metropolitan model was intensively used, that of the North Eastern model was doomed to inactivity. The full-size No. 13 was built at Darlington works in 1922 as an experimental high-speed 1,800 hp locomotive. It was carried on three driving-axles with driving-wheels 6ft 8in. in diameter and a four-wheel bogie at each end with 3ft 7¼in. wheels. The electrical equipment was supplied by Metropolitan-Vickers and consisted of three pairs of motors, each motor of 300 hp. The equipment included an electric boiler for generating the steam needed for heating the passenger-coaches. The total weight of the locomotive was 102 tons and its length over buffers 53ft 6in.

No. 13 was designed to haul a 450 ton-train at an average speed of 60 mph on straight level track, with a maximum permissible speed of 90 mph. The Shildon–Newport line, the first in Great Britain to be electrified on the 1,500 volt DC overhead system, was the venue of its trials. And here it performed to everyone's satisfaction, hauling a train of 460 tons up a gradient of 1 in 200 at 58 mph. But the electrification of the route for which it was really destined, the York–Newcastle main line, was never consummated.
Photo: Lent to Science Museum, London, by Lt.Col. J. P. Kennedy, North British Locomotive Co. Ltd and Metropolitan-Vickers Electrical Co. Ltd

India. In 1924 staff in the locomotive workshops at Jamalpur made this beautiful ¹⁄₁₂th scale-model of 5ft 6in. gauge East Indian Railway 2-8-0 goods engine No. 1588. It was presented to the Science Museum by the railway company. The full-size locomotive was one of a batch of 25 completed by the North British Locomotive Co. in 1923. The two 22in. × 26in. cylinders drove the third pair of 4ft 8½in. coupled wheels, the valve-gear being Walschaerts, which actuated piston valves. A Bissel truck was provided for the leading pair of 3ft 7in. wheels.

At 90 per cent of the working-pressure of 160lb./in.² the tractive effort was 32,070lb. The boiler diameter was 5ft 8½in. and length 12ft 6in., giving a total heating-surface of 2,082 sq. ft, of which the superheater accounted for 390 sq. ft and the Belpaire firebox 172 sq. ft. The grate-area was 32 sq. ft. The bogie tender held 4,500 gallons of water and 10 tons of coal. Total weight of engine and tender in working order was 138 tons, of which 66¼ tons were available for adhesion.
Photo: Crown Copyright. Science Museum, London
(top of facing page)

Eire. It is difficult to avoid superlatives where this model locomotive is concerned, either for the way in which its builder assiduously followed, in its design and construction, the same standards as were applied to the prototype, or for its perfection of detail and finish. The full-size engine, 4-6-0 No. 500 of the 5ft 3in. gauge Great Southern & Western Railway of Ireland, was built in 1924 to the designs of J. R. Bazin, the company's Chief Mechanical Engineer. Its two cylinders were 19½in. × 28in. and the coupled wheels 5ft 8½in., giving a tractive effort of 23,780lb. at 85 per cent of the boiler pressure of 180lb./in.². Total evaporative heating-surface was 1,772 sq. ft, supplemented by 440 sq. ft of the superheater, the grate-area being 28 sq. ft. Operational weight of the engine and tender was 161½ tons. Although No. 500 and sister engines Nos. 501 and 502 were originally intended for main-line goods traffic, they were found to be speedy and were soon at work hauling Dublin–Cork expresses.

Four years after the appearance of No. 500, C. R. H. Simpson of Gerrards Cross started the construction of a 1½in. to 1ft scale, 7½in. gauge replica. The first two years were spent on the preparation of detail drawings, the next 18 months on pattern making. Most of the patterns, which

took long to make, were used to produce only one casting. Similarly, many of the special cutters, gauges and flanging-blocks were made only to be used a few times. In some cases the components were cut from the solid. About 2 cwt of copper went into the construction of the 8in. diameter boiler, which was tested in steam to 200lb./in.². It has 27 flues of ⅝in. diameter and a grate-area of 60 sq. in. The fire-box has a brick arch, seldom to be found in working models. Construction of the tender, which holds 11¼ gallons of water and 65lb. of coal, absorbed 7lb. of ³⁄₃₂in. rivets and needed 96 leaves for the six laminated springs. In design the tender followed the GS&W 4,670 gallon-pattern, with no flared coping.

It was eventually decided not to steam the locomotive, so that corrosion of inaccessible places would never begin, but to present it to the Birmingham Museum of Science & Industry in mint condition. It must have been a difficult decision to make with a model which was probably capable of hauling 8 tons, and which had taken so many years to construct. For, with the period 1939–1945 as lost years, the model was not finally completed until 1967, 12 years after its prototype had made the final journey to the scrap-yard.
Photo: Birmingham Museum of Science & Industry

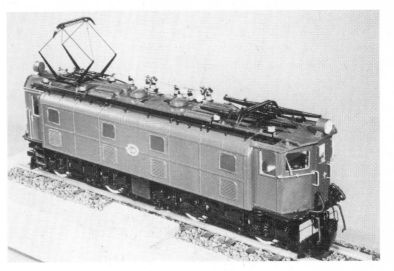

Hungary. A handsome working scale-model of Hungarian State Railways series 424 4-8-0 No. 245, photographed on the track in the city park of Hódmezővásárhely, in south Hungary. It is another example of the craftsmanship of Dr Alex Varga and was made by him to $\frac{1}{10}$th scale during the years 1938–1946.

The full-size locomotive was introduced by the Hungarian State Railways in 1924 for mixed-traffic duties that did not call for speeds higher than 85 kmph. The boiler, which had a normal firebox with an ample grate spread over the two rear pairs of coupled wheels, was given the extremely high centre-line of 10ft 10in. This was possible because of the liberal height of the Hungarian loading gauge. Two cylinders $23\frac{5}{8}$in. × 26in. were provided, actuating the second pair of 3ft 6in. coupled wheels. The fourth coupled axle had a side-play of $1\frac{1}{10}$in. either way and the bogie pivot was given a latitude of $2\frac{1}{8}$in. The total heating-surface was $1,740\frac{1}{5}$ sq. ft, to which the Schmidt superheater added $624\frac{3}{10}$ sq. ft, and the grate-area amounted to $47\frac{1}{5}$ sq. ft. The boiler-pressure was 191lb./in.^{2}, at 60 per cent of which the tractive effort was 22,848lb. Operational weight of engine and tender was 146 tons. Between 1924 and 1947 no less than 145 of these locomotives were constructed.
Photo: Dr Alex Varga

South Africa. Electrification of the Natal main line of the South African Railways between Glencoe and Pietermaritzburg was carried out during the years 1925–1927 and subsequently extended to Durban and Volksrust, with a branch to Harrismith. The 3,000 volt DC overhead system was adopted. A fleet of 78 1,200 hp Bo-Bo electric-locomotives, designated class 1E, was ordered in 1924 from Metropolitan-Vickers, which supplied a further 94 of the same general design up to the outbreak of World War II, the final three being classed 2E. The original batch had a length over buffers of 43ft 8in. and an operational weight of $66\frac{7}{10}$ tons. Their four 300 hp motors could produce a tractive effort of 21,200lb., the gear ratio being 17/75 and the maximum permissible speed 45 mph. The wheel diameter was 4ft and the total wheelbase 30ft 11in.

In 1938 ten class ES shunting locomotives from the same builders went into service. With the exception of the body their dimensions were identical with those of the 1E engines. Indeed, the traction-motors and bogies were interchangeable. H. Clarkson & Son made fully detailed replicas of both classes, Nos. E161 and E515 respectively, in 1959 for Metropolitan-Vickers. They were constructed to a scale of $\frac{1}{2}$in. to 1ft and are in the Railway Museum in Johannesburg.
Photo: H. Clarkson & Son

South Africa. An experimental 2-6-2+2-6-2 modified Fairlie-type locomotive was built in 1924 by the North British Co. (Works No. 23140) for the South African Railways, on which it became No. 2310 and the solitary occupant of class FC. Its four cylinders were 14in. × 23in. and its coupled wheels 3ft $6\frac{3}{4}$in. Total heating-surface was 1,387 sq. ft, the superheater-area being 280 sq. ft and grate-area 34 sq. ft. The boiler-pressure was 180lb./in.^{2}, at 75 per cent of which the tractive effort was 28,470lb., exactly the same as that of the class GC Beyer-Garratt engines of like wheel-arrangement, against which it was pitted. Unlike the Beyer-Garratts, however, the boiler, cab, water-tanks and coal-bunker were carried on one frame, beneath which the two groups of wheels, cylinders and motion were pivoted close to the centre of each unit.

After a life of only 15 years, No. 2310 (by then No. 670), went to the scrap-yard. The attractive $\frac{1}{12}$th scale-replica of this locomotive is in the Museum of Transport in Glasgow. The name of its maker does not appear to have survived.
Photo: Museum of Transport, Glasgow

Britain. Hafod Copper Works of Vivian & Sons Ltd at Swansea provided the venue for the first Beyer-Garratt locomotive to operate in Great Britain. Gradients of 1 in 20 and curves of 97ft radius called for an articulated engine, and in 1924 Beyer-Peacock & Co. provided an 0-4-0+0-4-0 which fulfilled all expectations with loads up to 150 tons. Fortunately for posterity, Captain Hugh Vivian had a sense of history and commissioned Twining Models Ltd to make a 1in. to 1ft scale-replica of the locomotive, which is reproduced. After his death his widow placed the model in the safekeeping of the Museum of Wales at Cardiff.

The prototype had four $13\frac{1}{2}$in. × 20in. cylinders and 3ft 4in. coupled wheels, steam-distribution being effected by Richardson balanced slide-valves worked by Walschaerts gear. The boiler had a diameter of 5ft and length of 9ft 6in., with a heating-surface of 1,299 sq. ft. The firebox had 107 sq. ft of heating-surface and a grate-area of $22\frac{7}{10}$ sq. ft. The working-pressure was 180lb./in.², at 75 per cent of which the tractive effort was 24,600lb. In working order the locomotive, No. 10 in the firm's books, weighed nearly $61\frac{1}{2}$ tons, including a full load of $1\frac{1}{2}$ tons of coal and 1,500 gallons of water. Its finish was black with vermilion bands lined gold, the injector pipes and chimney-cap being of polished copper.
Photo: Brian Monaghan

Sweden. When the Stockholm-Gothenburg main line of the Swedish State Railways was electrified in 1926, distinctive, wooden-bodied 1-C-1 locomotives of 1,660 hp made their appearance. They had been built by Asea and Falun the previous year. Known as class D, they had since become the most numerous type of locomotive in Sweden, 321 having been constructed between 1925 and 1943. Their coupled wheels are 5ft 0⅛in. in diameter and the weight in working order is 79½ tons. All-steel construction is now employed, although some wooden-bodied engines are still in service.

The first to be built, No. 101 has been restored and preserved in the Railway Museum at Gävle, where the splendid collection of models contains a $\frac{1}{10}$th scale reproduction of the same locomotive, which is illustrated. It was made in 1926 by the SJ Electrical Department.

Photo: Railway Museum, Gävle

Germany. Within a few years of the formation of the Deutsche Reichsbahn three standard Pacific type express-locomotives had been developed, classes 01 (two-cylinder simple) and 02 (four-cylinder compound) with a 20-ton axle-load and 03 (two-cylinder simple) with a 17-ton axle-load. A $\frac{1}{10}$th scale-model of the first named, No. 01.011, is to be seen in the museum at Nürnberg, and is reproduced. These engines had 23⅜in. × 26in. cylinders, 6ft 6$\frac{7}{10}$in. coupled wheels, a working pressure of 235lb./in.² and a tractive power of 41,890lb. They had 3,638 sq. ft of heating-surface and 48½ sq. ft of grate-area. With the tender the operational weight was 181⅜ tons. Seven German locomotive builders supplied class 01 engines over the years 1925–1940. They were Borsig, AEG, Schwartzkopff, Henschel, Maffei, Hohenzollern and Krupp.

Photo: Verkehrsmuseum, Nürnberg

U.S.A. What are generally considered to be the first commercially successful diesel-electric (then called oil-electric) locomotives in the United States were the result of a combined effort of American Locomotive Co., General Electric Co. and Ingersoll-Rand in 1925. Together they produced three similar double-bogie 60 ton units, each 32ft in length and carried on 2ft 2in. diameter wheels. The power-equipment consisted of an Ingersoll-Rand 300hp oil-engine directly connected to a General Electric 200 kw generator. Motive-power was provided by four HM-840 motors, one of which was geared to each of the four axles.

The locomotives were sold to the Central of New Jersey, Lehigh Valley and Baltimore & Ohio Railroads, on all of which they went into yard service. The Smithsonian Institution displays a model of the first-named, built to a scale of 1in. to 1ft.
Photo: Smithsonian Institution, Washington

Nigeria. Nearly 6ft long overall, this $\frac{1}{12}$th scale-model of Nigerian Railway 2-8-2 freight locomotive No. 801, built in 1925 by Vulcan Foundry Ltd, was to be seen in the Nigerian Pavilion at the Wembley Exhibition that year. It was made by Bassett-Lowke Ltd, its massive mahogany stand concealing an electric-motor which would actuate the coupled wheels and valve-motion.

The prototype, which operated on the 3ft 6in. gauge, had three cylinders 18in. × 28in., coupled wheels 4ft 6in. and a working pressure of 180lb./in.², which produced a tractive effort of 40,825lb. The large boiler was given an inside diameter of 5ft 5$\frac{3}{4}$in. and a length of 22ft 5in. The evaporative heating-surface amounted to 2,290 sq. ft, to which the firebox contributed 210 sq. ft. The superheater-surface was 506 sq. ft and the grate-area 38 sq. ft. Weight in working order of engine and its double-bogie tender, which held 3,000 gallons of water and 7$\frac{1}{2}$ tons of coal ,was 126 tons. No. 801 was soon named *Sir Hugh Clifford* after the Governor of Nigeria.
Photo: Bassett-Lowke Ltd

Switzerland. In the summer of 1925 the Bern–Lötschberg–Simplon Railway put into service two handsome 1-Co-Co-1 electric locomotives that were the most powerful single-phase (15,000 volts 16⅔ periods) railway-units in the world. They were capable of hauling loads of 600 tons up 27 per cent gradients at 55 kmph. The Sécheron Works of Geneva designed them and manufactured the electrical equipment, the remainder being supplied by Ernesto Breda of Milan. Rated at 4,000 hp, their special feature was the use of individually driven axles in conjunction with a flexible motor-drive to driving-wheels having a comparatively small diameter of 4ft 5in. The latter made it possible to achieve the high power-output and drawbar-pull stipulated. With an overall length of 66ft 6in. and a gross weight of 138.4 tons the weight per horsepower-output was only 31.4 kg.

These locomotives were designated class Be 6/8. They were so much ahead of their time that it was possible, in 1939, to rebuild them with the object of increasing the top speed from 75 kmph to 90 kmph. Further modification in 1960 raised the maximum speed to 100 kmph, when they were redesignated class Ae 6/8. Their equipment includes rheostatic brakes. The Swiss Transport Museum model illustrated is made to a scale of $\frac{1}{10}$th and faithfully reproduces No. 210 of the class as originally built.

Photo: Swiss Transport Museum, Lucerne

Sweden. An exquisite little 7mm. scale-model, 1¼in. gauge, of class U (later Ua) O-C-O electric shunting locomotive No. 89 of the Swedish State Railways. It was made in 1970 by H. Clarkson & Son for the Gothenburg Model Railway Society.

The prototype was one of three (Nos. 88–90) delivered in 1926 by Nydqvist & Holm and Asea. Weighing 46½ tons, it had a length over buffers of 31ft 6in. and its coupled wheels were 3ft 7$\frac{3}{10}$in. in diameter. The one traction-motor was of 700hp and the locomotive was designed for a maximum speed of 45 kmph.

Photo: H. Clarkson & Son

Australia. Although there was an interval of 25 years between the appearance of the first, rather oddly designated, B $18\frac{1}{4}$ and BB $18\frac{1}{4}$ mixed traffic Pacific locomotives of the 3ft 6in. gauge Queensland Railways, they can conveniently be dealt with together. Almost all the leading dimensions were the same and there was comparatively little difference in external appearance, especially when the earliest engines had been equipped with the improvements enjoyed by those built later. The first B $18\frac{1}{4}$ engines were completed in 1926 at the Ipswich works of the Queensland Railways and introduced the Pacific wheel-arrangement. Altogether 83 were constructed, either at Ipswich or by Walkers Ltd, a Queensland firm, the last entering service as late as 1947. Originally intended for the haulage of express passenger and mail trains, the B $18\frac{1}{4}$ eventually became a maid-of-all-work. Its two cylinders were $18\frac{1}{4}$in. $\times$ 24in. and the coupled wheels 4ft 3in. Total heating surface was 1,957 sq. ft and the grate-area 25 sq. ft. At 85 per cent of the 170 (originally 160)lb./in.^{2} boiler-pressure the tractive effort was 22,648 lb. The tender capacity was either 3,000 gallons of water and 8 tons of coal or 3,050 gallons and 7 tons 7 cwt, the operational weight of locomotive and tender being $93\frac{1}{4}$ tons or $91\frac{7}{10}$ tons respectively.

The BB $18\frac{1}{4}$ class appeared in 1951, when 35 were completed at the Vulcan Foundry. Four years later a further 20 were constructed by Walkers Ltd, the last order for steam-locomotives to be fulfilled in Australia. They were given increased fuel capacity, the tender holding 3,500 gallons of water and 10 tons 7 cwt of coal, and the overall length was 1ft $6\frac{3}{8}$in. greater at 60ft $2\frac{7}{8}$in. In consequence, the operational weight was heavier at $101\frac{1}{5}$ tons. Increased valve-travel, side bearer type spring-controlled leading bogies and roller-bearing axleboxes on all axles were among the new features. The tender tanks were of welded and riveted construction.

In 1933 William Olds of Maryborough completed a 5in. gauge $1\frac{7}{16}$in. to 1ft scale-model of class B $18\frac{1}{4}$ No. 830. It was a wonderful performer and at various shows demonstrated its ability to haul seven flat wagons carrying up to 60 children at a time on a 67ft diameter track. It was sold in 1934 to showmen and immediately afterwards Olds began to build a second engine to the same scale, but it was not completed until 1945. Then this, too, was sold to showmen. Today, after many vicissitudes, both model locomotives are back at Maryborough, having been restored to their present pristine condition by Peter Olds, son of their maker. Both are finished in the correct livery of hawthorn green, lined-out black and red, and afford accurate replicas of class B $18\frac{1}{4}$ No. 830 as originally built and class BB $18\frac{1}{4}$ No. 860.

The names by which the two engines have always been known, *Polly* and *Sally*, have never been carried on the customary nameplates. But now each name appears over the leading buffer-beam in the place where a destination board was normally displayed when the prototype headed suburban trains. *Polly*, owned by Peter Olds, and *Sally*, which belongs to Brian Fogarty, are in regular use, giving happiness to the hordes of children who, almost invariably, form their loads.

Photos: R. J. Olds

Switzerland. The 2,240 hp class Ce 6/8[III] freight-locomotive was the last Swiss Federal Railways design to embody coupling-rods for transmission of the drive of the motors to the axles. It was originally introduced for handling freight trains on the Gotthard line and its feeders. It is an impressive locomotive, beautifully captured by the $\frac{1}{10}$th scale-model of No. 14318 in the Swiss Transport Museum.

Oerlikon Engineering Works and Swiss Locomotive Works delivered the first batch in 1926–1927. To assist negotiation of curves, the locomotives were carried on two 8-wheeled bogies, with two traction-motors to each bogie, their power being transmitted by means of gearing to a common counter-shaft, thence to the two inner pairs of coupled wheels by traverse side-rods. Each locomotive was equipped with regenerative braking and weighed 128 tons in working order. Some of them were subsequently rebuilt to class Be 6/8[III] of 2,460 hp, raising the weight to 131 tons and the maximum speed from 65 to 75 kmph. The remainder were refitted with 3,640 hp motors and the top speed likewise raised to 75 kmph. They now mainly work in the more level country of central Switzerland and the Jura.

Photo: Swiss Transport Museum, Lucerne

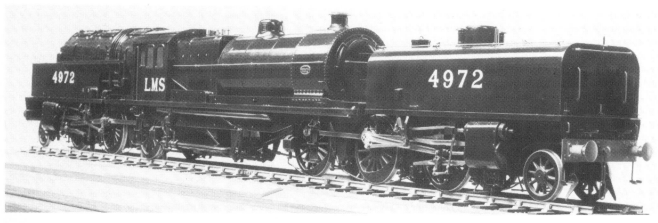

Britain. Crewe Apprentices School made this $\frac{3}{4}$in. to 1 ft scale-model of London, Midland & Scottish 2-6-0 + 0-6-2 Beyer-Garratt in 1962–1963 for the Museum of British Transport. The LMS was the only British railway to use Beyer-Garratts on a large scale. They were designed specifically for the haulage of heavy South Yorkshire coal-traffic from Toton marshalling yard to London, a distance of 126½ miles, in order to eliminate double-heading. After successful trials with three of these engines, Nos. 4997–4999 built by Beyer-Peacock in 1927, a further 30 (Nos. 4967–4996) were constructed in 1930. In addition to saving one set of enginemen per train they displaced 68 old tender-engines.

They were powerful locomotives, having a tractive effort of 45,620 lb at 85 per cent of the boiler-pressure, and comfortably handled trains of 1,500 tons. The four cylinders were 18½in. × 26in. and coupled wheels 5ft 3in. The working-pressure was 190lb./in.[2] and total evaporative heating-surface 2,137 sq. ft, the superheater having 466 sq. ft of heating-surface. The grate-area was 44½ sq. ft. The model embodies a replica of the self-trimming coal bunker with which No. 4972 and others of the class were subsequently equipped. This was a closed conical container, inclined towards the footplate and revolved by power, so bringing forward the coal (of which it held 9 tons) as needed. The water capacity was 4,500 gallons and the total weight in working order 152½ tons.

Photo: Philip J. Kelley

Morocco. The Moroccan Railways are now operated by the State-established Office National des Chemins de Fer (ONCF). They are formed of a compact system of over 1,100 miles, with a main-line from Marrakesh through Casablanca and Rabat and eastwards over part of the Tangier–Fez Railway to join the Algerian Railways beyond Ouja. Electric traction by overhead line at 3,000 volts DC was inaugurated in 1927 and now extends over much of the system. Mixed traffic B-B locomotives were introduced, of which there is an excellent $\frac{1}{10}$th scale-model—of No. E601—in the Musée des Techniques in Paris.

The 1,200 hp prototype was built by Cie Constructions Electriques de France, being similar to a 1922 design of the Midi Railway. Nose-suspended motors, two to each bogie, are embodied and the equipment includes regenerative braking. The locomotive is capable of a speed of 90 kmph.
Photo: Musée des Techniques CNAM, Paris

Italy. One of the numerous class 626 Bo-Bo-Bo 3,000 volt DC mixed traffic electric locomotives of the Italian State Railways is represented by this $\frac{1}{20}$th scale-model. The first appeared in 1927, when a large measure of standardisation was initiated. Design stipulations met were a maximum tractive effort of 39,683 lb (18,000 Kg) at 40 kmph, a maximum axle-load of 15¾ tons and a maximum speed of 90 kmph. The three bogies carry six nose-suspended motors and run on 4ft 1in. wheels. Draw and buffing gear are fixed to the bogie frames and such loads are not transmitted to the body. The electrical equipment is housed at each end, in front of the cab, and in a central engine-room. In working order the weight of the locomotive is 91½ tons.
Photo: Museo Nazionale della Scienza e della Tecnica Leonardo da Vinci, Milan

Angola. The first Beyer-Garratts of the 4-8-2 + 2-8-4 wheel arrangement, and the then largest to operate on 60lb rail, were built in 1927 by Beyer Peacock & Co. Ltd for the 3ft 6in. gauge Benguela Railway. This line traverses Angola from the Atlantic coast at Lobito to the Katanga frontier at Dilolo and was completed throughout, a distance of 838 miles, in 1928. When the Bas Congo–Katanga Railways were extended to Dilolo three years later the Benguela began to fulfil its conception as an outlet for the Katanga copper-mines. Six Beyer-Garratts were first ordered. Their four cylinders were 18½in. × 24in. and the coupled wheels were 4ft in diameter. Total heating-surface was 3,014 sq. ft and the grate-area 51½ sq. ft. At 85 per cent of the boiler-pressure of 180lb./in.² the tractive effort was 52,360lb. Total weight in working order was just under 168½ tons.

These engines were given a hard gruelling for two years on the most severe section of the line, between San Pedro and Huambo, which has a ruling gradient of 1 in 40 and curves of 300ft radius. They were highly successful and were followed by 14, with bar instead of plate frames, in 1930. Yet another 28 of the same wheel-arrangement were delivered during 1951–1955. The beautiful model illustrated is of No. 302 of 1927. It was made by Bassett-Lowke Ltd and its wheels and valve-gear can be set in motion by an electric-motor concealed in the base of its showcase.
Photo: Bassett-Lowke Ltd

Canada. Some of the most successful of all Canadian dual-purpose locomotives were the class U-2-a Northern or 4-8-4 engines of the Canadian National Railways. The first, No. 6100, emerged from Kingston Locomotive Works in 1927, only six months after the first American locomotive of this wheel-arrangement had been produced by the Northern Pacific. On the Canadian National it was better known as the Confederation type, because of its appearance, almost to the day, on the sixtieth anniversary of that event. Forty of these engines, at the time the most powerful in the British Empire, initially went into service at the head of fast and heavy sixteen-car expresses between Montreal, Toronto, Sarnia and other centres. Ten of them, built by the Canadian Locomotive Co., were equipped with boosters which actuated the rear pair of wheels on the trailing bogie.

The U-2-as had $25\frac{1}{2}$in. × 30in. cylinders, 6ft 1in. coupled wheels and a working-pressure of 250lb./in.^{2}. The heating-surface was made up of 3,814 sq. ft by the tubes, 117 sq. ft by the superheater and 315 sq. ft by the firebox, the grate-area being $84\frac{2}{5}$ sq. ft. Feed-water heaters and mechanical stokers were provided. Inclusion of a booster had the following effects upon weights and power output:

Weights:	*With booster*	*Without booster*
On coupled wheels	$103\frac{3}{4}$ tons	$102\frac{3}{4}$ tons
On leading bogie	29 tons	29 tons
On trailing bogie	$40\frac{1}{2}$ tons	37 tons
Total	$173\frac{1}{4}$ tons	$168\frac{3}{4}$ tons
Tractive effort	67,700 lb	56,800 lb

The 12-wheeled Vanderbilt-type tender, with 11,300 gallons of water and 20 tons of coal, weighed 116 tons, so that the working order weight of engine and tender was in excess of 280 tons.

A well-finished $\frac{1}{4}$in. fine scale-model of No. 6100, made specially in Japan for James Plomer of Milford, Ontario, represents the class. It is motorised and runs on $1\frac{1}{4}$in. gauge track, two-rail electric, 12-volt DC or 18-volt AC. Its construction is of heavy-gauge brass. All axles are sprung and the driver-springs are compensated, which results in such excellent riding-qualities that the locomotive never derails, even on rough track. It can negotiate curves of 5ft 6in. radius and is capable of hauling ten scale-model 80ft passenger-cars on the level.
Photo: James Plomer

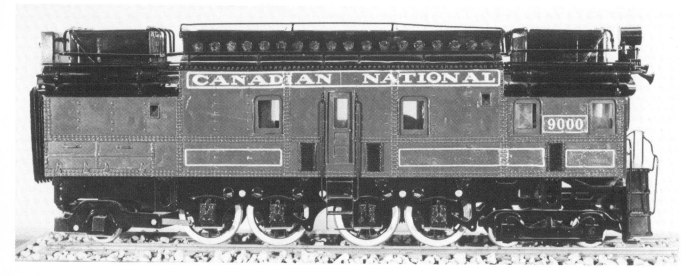

U.S.A. An impressive model of New York Central 4-6-4 express locomotive No. 5205 built by Severn-Lamb Ltd to a scale of ½in. to 1ft for the Smithsonian Institution. Its full-size prototype was completed in the Schenectady workshops of the American Locomotive Co. in 1927 and went into service hauling the heaviest and fastest passenger-trains such as the *Twentieth Century Limited* and *Empire State Express*. It was the first Baltic or 4-6-4 tender engine design to appear on an American railway. The New York Central designated it the Hudson type.

Because of the attention given to detail, it was a much tidier looking locomotive than most of its contemporaries. For example, piping was simplified and rendered inconspicuous, sometimes being concealed by external casing. The feed-water heater was carried in a depression in the upper part of the smokebox in the current German fashion. In the cab, all gauges, save those for the air and back pressure, were mounted on one common instrument-board.

The trailing bogie incorporated a booster, an auxiliary engine giving extra power on starting, when it added 10,900lb. to the 42,300lb. tractive effort of the main engine. Cylinders were 25in. × 28in. and the evenly spaced coupled wheels 6ft 7in. in diameter. The boiler-pressure was 225lb./in.² and the total heating-surface of the boiler amounted to 4,484 sq. ft, the grate-area being 81½ sq. ft. With its tender, which held 10,000 gallons of water and 17 tons of soft coal, the New York Central Hudson weighed 315 tons.
Photo: Severn-Lamb Ltd

Canada. The first diesel-electric locomotive to run on Canadian metals, as distinct from a diesel-powered railcar, was No. 9000 of the Canadian National Railways. It was built in 1928 by the Canadian Locomotive Co. at Kingston, being put into traffic on 26 September 1929 with a sister engine No. 9001. Both were powered by 1500 hp Beardmore V-12 engines.

After they had been in passenger and freight service for 11 years in Quebec and Ontario, No. 9001 was withdrawn. No. 9000 was rebuilt at Winnipeg for duties on the west coast during the war years and, unfortunately, was not preserved when it was taken out of traffic some 15 months after the end of hostilities. Its likeness, however, has been preserved for posterity in the ½in. to 1ft scale-model illustrated. This is on display in the Ontario Science Centre and was made by F. Jerome of Toronto.
Photo: Ontario Science Centre, Don Mills

Britain. Completed in 1929 and originally dubbed the *Hush-Hush* locomotive because of the conditions of secrecy under which it was built at the Darlington works of the London & North Eastern Railway, No. 10000 was unique in several respects. It is fortunate, therefore, that a perfect 1in. to 1ft scale-model of such an engine is in existence. It was made at the Doncaster works of the LNER for the Brussels Exhibition of 1934 and is now on permanent loan to the County Borough Museum of Darlington. The primary object of No. 10000, an experimental locomotive, was to achieve economy, not greater power. It was conceived in 1924, when H. N. Gresley and Harold Yarrow initiated the development of a water-tube boiler for application to locomotives. The Yarrow-Gresley boiler was patented three years later and was followed by experiments by Gresley and Professor W. E. Dalby of the City & Guilds Technical College to solve problems of smoke deflection under all kinds of weather and wind conditions. These were called for by the profile which the shape of the boiler dictated.

When No. 10000 appeared it created a sensation, which the author can vividly recall, for nothing like it had been seen before. It was a complete departure from normal British practice, with its marine-type boiler, unprecedented working-pressure of 450lb./in.², four cylinders designed for compound working, and semi-streamlined form. Its battleship-grey, chromium-banded bulk (which earned it another nickname, *Galloping Sausage*) and the fact that it was the first (and only) British 4-6-4 tender-engine added

further piquancy to its impact. Save for the extra pair of trailing wheels mounted on a Bissel truck, the wheel-spacing and diameters were the same as those of Gresley's standard Pacifics, the coupled wheels being 6ft 8in. The two inside high-pressure 12in. (soon altered to 10in.) × 26in. cylinders drove the leading pair of coupled wheels and the outside low-pressure 20in. × 26in. cylinders the middle pair. Thus the tractive effort at 85 per cent of the boiler-pressure was 32,000lb. Two sets of Walschaerts motion actuated the outside piston-valves in the usual way, connexion being made to the inside valve-spindles by means of rocking-shafts. The total evaporative heating-surface was made up of 919 sq. ft by the firebox, 195 sq. ft by the combustion-chamber and 872 sq. ft by the small tubes. The 12-element super-heater had a heating-surface of 140 sq. ft. A standard corridor tender holding 5,000 gallons of water and nine tons of coal was provided, making the operational weight of engine and tender 166 tons.

In regular service, hauling the principal East Coast expresses, including the non-stop *Flying Scotsman*, the water-tube boiler proved to be too revolutionary. But the smoke-deflection arrangement was successful and was the forerunner of the distinctive wedge-shape front end adopted for the class A4 streamlined Pacifics. No. 10000 was rebuilt in 1937 as a three-cylinder simple 4-6-4 with normal boiler generally similar to the A4s and finished in the same beautiful blue livery.

Photo: County Borough Museum of Darlington

South Africa. At the time of their appearance on the Pieter-maritzburg–Durban section of the South African Railways in 1929, the class GL 4-8-2 + 2-8-4 Beyer-Garratts were the most powerful steam-locomotives in operation in the southern hemisphere. At 85 per cent of the boiler-pressure their tractive effort was 78,650 lb. The four cylinders were 22in. × 26in., the coupled wheels 4ft and the working-pressure 200lb./in.². The total heating-surface was 3,049 sq. ft and the firebox, which was equipped with two Nicholson thermic syphons, added 374 sq. ft more. The superheater-area was 835 sq. ft and the grate-area 75 sq. ft. Needless to say, a mechanical stoker was provided. In working order these enormous engines, which measured 90ft 7⅞in. over buffer-faces, weighed 211 tons 1 cwt, including a full bunker of 12 tons of coal and tanks holding 7,000 gallons of water.

Bassett–Lowke Ltd made the 10mm. to 1ft scale-model of No. 2350 illustrated for Beyer Peacock & Co. in 1954. It embodied the steam-operated cowls on the chimney with which the prototype and its sisters were subsequently equipped because of the several tunnels on the line between Durban and Cato Ridge.
Photo: Bassett–Lowke Ltd

Canada. A heavy-duty switching and hump yard locomotive design is represented by this ¾in. to 1ft working scale-model of Canadian Pacific 0-8-0 No. 6608. It was built by Jack Hewitson in 1958 and is owned by W. Kent of Vancouver. The model weighs 125 lb in working order and measures 4ft 8in. overall in length, the boiler-pressure being 90lb./in.². Its equipment includes superheater, piston-valves and mechanical lubricator.

Its prototype was built in 1930 with 22½in. × 32in. cylinders and 4ft 10in. coupled wheels. The boiler-pressure was 250lb./in.² and weight in working order 256 tons.
Photo: Jack Hewitson

Britain. This beautifully finished, coal-fired, 7¼in. gauge scale-model of Great Western class 4700 2-8-0 mixed-traffic locomotive No. 4701 was completed in 1970 by K. E. Wilson of Winkleigh and is owned by J. F. Hall-Craggs of Brightwalton. It makes a welcome change from the never-ending procession of *Kings*, *Castles*, Dean bogie singles and pannier tanks with which so many modelling devotees of Swindon seem to be obsessed nowadays, to the exclusion of all else. The fully brazed or silver-soldered copper boiler embodies 24 ⅝in.-diameter firetubes and has been tested hydraulically to 200lb./in.² It has a readily accessible blow-down and drain plug in the cab, while the twin safety-valve combination, although of correct pattern, is easily removed for valve oiling and inspection. The front section of the grate and ashpan can be removed by withdrawing a pin. The 2½in. × 3in. cylinders are of fine-grain cast iron, the bores being hone finish. The correct inside Stephenson's link-motion is fitted.

External details of the prototype have been faithfully reproduced, on both the engine and tender. The latter has a screw-operated handbrake and the engine a steam-brake acting on the coupled wheels. The brake hangers can be withdrawn without dismantling the brake-gear.

When the Great Western introduced the prototype in 1919 it was the first eight-coupled mixed-traffic locomotive in Britain. It was later provided with the larger boiler and tender which are reproduced in the model. In this condition the total heating surface was increased to 2,521 ⁷⁄₁₀ sq. ft, the grate-area to 30⅙ sq. ft and the operational weight of the engine and tender to 128 ⁷⁄₁₀ tons. With 19in. × 30in. cylinders, 5ft 8in. coupled wheels and a working-pressure of 225lb./in.² the tractive-effort was 30,460lb.
Photo: J. F. Hall-Craggs

PLATE IX

Britain. Twining Models Ltd made this handsome replica of a class S69 express passenger 4-6-0 of the Great Eastern Railway for William Beardmore & Co. Ltd of Glasgow in 1921, the year the firm completed the prototype and 19 others, Nos. 1541–1560. The model is exhibited in the Museum of Transport in Glasgow; its scale is 1in. to 1ft.

The first S69 engines appeared in 1912 and in many respects their form was akin to that of the handsome *Claud Hamilton* 4-4-0 introduced earlier by James Holden. The cab was one of the most capacious ever provided for a British locomotive. The tender was, however, somewhat diminutive and held only 3,700 gallons of water and 4 tons of coal; so many 50ft-diameter turntables were still in use that the total wheelbase of the engine and tender had to be kept down to 48ft 3in. Cylinders were 20in. × 28in. and the coupled wheels 6ft 6in. The boiler, 5ft 1⅛in. in diameter and 12ft 6in. in length, provided 1,489 sq. ft of heating-surface, to which the Schmidt superheater added 286⅔ sq. ft and the Belpaire firebox 143½ sq. ft. The grate area was 26½ sq. ft. With a working pressure of 180lb./in.² the tractive effort was 21,970lb. and the operational weight of the engine and tender 101¼ tons.

Photo: Museum of Transport, Glasgow

PLATE X

Switzerland. With the conversion of the Bodensee-Toggenburg Railway to electric working in the 1930s, a 1600 hp lightweight medium-duty locomotive, carried on bogies, was developed and built during the years 1931–1932 by the Swiss Locomotive & Machine Works in co-operation with Sécheron. The outcome is depicted by this Swiss Transport Museum model made to $\frac{1}{10}$th scale in the Herisau workshops of the railway company.

This type of electric locomotive, known as class Be 4/4, has rendered excellent service hauling medium loads on lines having gradients not exceeding 28 per cent. Its weight in working order is 62 tons and its maximum speed 80 kmph. Sécheron spring-band coupling, as used on the class Be 6/8 locomotives of the Bern–Lotschberg-Simplon, and Sécheron switchgear are included in the equipment. Similar locomotives, differing only in minor changes in design, were adopted by the Emmental–Burgdorf–Thun and Solothurn–Munster Railways.

Photo: Swiss Transport Museum, Lucerne

France. Super-Pacifics of the Northern Railway of France (Chemin de fer du Nord) were so-called to distinguish them from predecessors of the same wheel-arrangement. Introduced in 1923, they soon became well-known to travellers between Calais and Paris. They operated with great regularity and economy some of the heaviest and fastest trains in Europe, handling loads of 500–600 metric tons at speeds of 90–110 kmph. Fifty were in use (Nos. 3.1201–3.1250), when a further 40, Nos. 3.1251–3.1290, were ordered from various builders in 1931. The model depicts the first of this latter batch, No. 3.1251. It was obtained in the French secondhand market by G. P. Keen, President of the Model Railway Club. His words, 'after much refurbishing and being fitted with a hotted-up Permag electric-motor it runs well', modestly describe a most competent job of reconstruction. The result was the creation of a 7mm. to 1ft fully detailed scale working model of an impressive prototype.

The Nord Super-Pacifics were four-cylinder compounds on the de Glehn-du Bousquet system. The drive was divided; the leading pair of 6ft $2\frac{1}{3}$in. coupled wheels were actuated by the inside $17\frac{1}{3}$in. × 26in. high-pressure cylinders; and the middle pair by the outside $24\frac{2}{3}$in. × $27\frac{1}{3}$in. low-pressure cylinders. The valve gear was Walschaerts, independent and separately controlled for high-pressure and low-pressure units, so permitting the locomotive to be worked temporarily as a four-cylinder simple. A Belpaire firebox was embodied in the boiler and the total heating-surface, including the superheater, amounted to 1,851 sq. ft, the grate-area being $37\frac{7}{10}$ sq. ft. The working-pressure was 227lb./in.². As a compound the tractive effort was 37,830lb and as a simple 50,771lb. The double-bogie tender had a water capacity of 1,307 cu ft and carried nine tons of coal. Engine and tender weighed 175 tons in working order.

Photo: G. P. Keen

U.S.S.R. The best proportioned of the Russian heavy freight locomotives is the class FD 2-10-2, its clean lines being assisted by the absence of the deck-type handrails favoured by so many of its predecessors. Its design embodied the typical clerestory cab skylight and several American features, including bar frames, mechanical stoker and thermic syphons. Voroshilovgrad works (formerly, and now again, Lugansk works), then only recently rebuilt, turned out the first in 1931. They were the forerunners of 3,000 more constructed there in the next seven years. Most are still in service on non-electrified lines of heavy traffic density.

They were given 4ft 11in. coupled wheels, two cylinders $26\frac{3}{10}$in. $\times$ 30in. and a boiler-pressure of 220lb./in.². The grate-area is $75\frac{3}{10}$ sq. ft and the weight in working order 134 tons, of which 101 tons are available for adhesion. The 12-wheeled tender holds 25 tons of coal and 11,600 gallons of water. The splendid $\frac{1}{10}$th scale-model of No. 20–05 is displayed in the USSR Railways Museum. It was made in 1939 by the teaching and manufacturing workshops of the

NKPS Technical School in Rostov.
Photo: USSR Railways

U.S.S.R. The class IS–20 (Iosif Stalin) 2-8-4 locomotive of the Russian railways is represented in the USSR Railways Museum by this scale-model of No. 20–1. It is the passenger equivalent of the freight class FD 2-10-2. Kolomna works, in collaboration with those at Izhogorski, built the first engines in 1932. They were allocated to the haulage of the *Red Arrow* expresses over the October Railway between Moscow and Leningrad. Mass production of the class was undertaken at the Lugansk works.

These locomotives have two cylinders $26\frac{3}{8}$in. $\times$ $30\frac{3}{8}$in., 6ft $\frac{7}{8}$in. coupled wheels and a working-pressure of 220lb./in.². The heating-surface is 3,177 sq. ft, supplemented by 1,597 sq. ft superheater-surface, the grate-area being $75\frac{1}{8}$ sq. ft. They weigh 133 tons, with 81 tons adhesive. Their tractive effort is some 60,000lb and designed speed 115kmph.
Photo: USSR Railways

France. Among the more creditable long-distance high-speed runs of the 1930s was that of the *Sud Express* of the Paris–Orleans and Midi systems. It accomplished the 451 miles from Paris to Dax at an average speed of 56mph. For working this train and other 650 ton expresses on its fastest schedules the Midi introduced six large 2-D-2 electric-locomotives at the end of 1932. An excellent model of one of them, No. E4801, is displayed in the Musée des Techniques in Paris. It was made to $\frac{1}{10}$th scale and is fully detailed externally. It carries the initials SNCF of its final owner, the French Railways.

These locomotives were built by Cie Construction Electriques de France for working on 1,500 volts DC, each having a continuous capacity of 3,200 hp. The motors were entirely spring-borne, the design of the drive and that of the locomotives generally being largely influenced by experience with earlier 2,100 hp 2-C-2s.

The length of these locomotives was 55ft 2in. over buffers and their weight in working order 120 tons, of which 75 tons was available for adhesion. The tractive effort was 50,000 lb.

Photo: Musée des Techniques CNAM, Paris

U.S.S.R. The class SO 2-10-0 freight-locomotive of the USSR Railways was introduced in 1934. It had plate frames, two cylinders 25½in. × 27½in., coupled wheels 4ft 4in. and a boiler-pressure of 206lb./in.². The total heating-surface was 2,443 sq. ft, the superheater-surface 1,044 sq. ft and the grate-area 64½ sq. ft. All but ten tons of its operational weight of 104 tons were available for adhesion.

Series SO–19, constructed over the years 1936–1941 in the Kharkov, Briansk and Lugansk works, were equipped with a condensation system for working on lines in Asiatic Russia lacking water-supplies. This called for the provision of special condenser-vans, which were built at the Kolomna works. A model of one of these engines, complete with condenser-van, is to be seen in the USSR Railways Museum. It was made in the 1940s to a scale of 1/10th.
Photo: USSR Railways

China. This handsome 1/20th full-size model of a Chinese National Railways 4ft 8½in. gauge 4-8-4 mixed-traffic locomotive was made by Bassett-Lowke Ltd for the Vulcan Foundry Ltd of Newton-le-Willows in 1936. It was exhibited that year at the British Industries Fair at Olympia, London. Mounted on electrically operated rollers, the coupled wheels and Walschaerts gear could be set in motion at a realistic speed. The model faithfully reproduced one of the 24 locomotives, the largest then built by Vulcan, which were ordered by the Chinese Government Purchasing Commission in 1934–1935. Sixteen were allotted to the Canton–Hankow trunk route and the remainder to the busy Nanking–Shanghai line.

Length of the engine and tender overall was 93ft 2½in. Coupled wheels were 5ft 9in., leading bogie wheels 3ft ¼in. and trailing bogie wheels 3ft 7¼in. in diameter. The two cylinders of the first 16 locomotives were 20⅞in. × 29½in. and of the last eight 21¼in. × 29½in. The tapered boiler had a working-pressure of 220½lb./in.², its heating-surface combined with that of the superheater being 3,724 sq. ft. Because of the poor coal burned by these engines they were provided with generous fireboxes having a total heating-surface of 340 sq. ft, the fuel being fed in by a mechanical stoker. The engine for the latter was carried by the 12-wheeled tender, which also held 11¾ tons of coal and 6,600 gallons of water. The tractive effort of these locomotives was 32,920lb and, with their tenders, each weighed 192 tons 14½ cwt in working order.
Photo: Bassett–Lowke Ltd

U.S.A. This Smithsonian Institution model of Baltimore & Ohio Railroad locomotive No. 50 depicts, in a scale of $\frac{1}{2}$in to 1ft, what is regarded as the first diesel-electric passenger-locomotive to operate on a railway in the United States.

The prototype was built in 1935 by General Motors Corporation to the design of Charles F. Kettering. It was powered by two 201-A, V-12 two-cycle engines producing 1,800 hp and housed in a coach-type body. No. 50 was capable of hauling trains of standard passenger-cars and remained in service until 1956.
Photo: Smithsonian Institution, Washington

U.S.A. An industrial designer, Raymond Loewy, was responsible for the external styling of the class GG1 2-C + C-2 electric locomotives of the Pennsylvania Railroad, which have a distinctive appearance of their own. The first series, Nos. 4801–4856, originally designed for through passenger-train working between New York and Washington and between Philadelphia and Harrisburg, were turned out in 1935. Some were assembled by the Altoona shops of the PRR and some by outside builders, the electrical equipment being provided by Westinghouse.

These engines operate on 11,000 volts AC, single phase. Their driving-wheels are 4ft 9in. and they were originally geared for a top speed of 90 mph. They are rated at 4,500 hp and weigh 205 tons. Most are still in use, engaged on freight-train services. The Smithsonian Institution model of No. 4801, made to a scale of $\frac{3}{4}$in. to 1ft, faithfully reproduces all the external characteristics of the design.
Photo: Smithsonian Institution, Washington

U.S.S.R. This $\frac{1}{20}$th scale-model locomotive in the USSR Railways Museum was made in Leningrad as recently as 1972 by the Combine of Decorative & Applied Arts & Sculpture of the Artists Foundation. It portrays No. 221–70, one of the third series of some 500 class Su 2-6-2s which were built in 1935–1940.

The first Su engines were constructed in 1925 at Kolomna works to meet an urgent need for a modern passenger-locomotive. Some were fitted to burn oil. All were two-cylinder machines, their equipment including Tchousoff superheaters, Trofimoff piston-valves and hollow axles. The leading pony truck, embodying 3ft 5$\frac{3}{8}$in. wheels, was a Kolomna derivation of the well-known Krauss-Helmholtz type; the trailing truck, with 4ft 4in. wheels, was of Bissel pattern. Coupled wheels of the Su class are 6ft $\frac{7}{8}$in., the cylinders 22$\frac{3}{8}$in. × 27$\frac{1}{2}$in. and the working-pressure 185 lb./in.². The grate-area amounts to 51$\frac{3}{4}$ sq. ft and to the total heating-surface of 2,974$\frac{4}{5}$ sq. ft the Belpaire firebox contributes 199$\frac{1}{10}$ sq. ft and the superheater 785$\frac{1}{10}$ sq. ft. Working-order weight of the engine and tender is 147 metric tons.

Some 400 of the first series were built and they can be readily distinguished from later batches by their moulded cast-iron chimneys with rather heavy rims. A second series of about 1,000 locomotives was taken in hand in 1932 and a fourth during 1947–1950. The locomotive works at Kolomna, Sormovsk, Lugansk, Briansk and Kharkov have all had a share in the construction of the Su class, which still forms the backbone of the steam passenger-locomotive stud.
Photo: USSR Railways

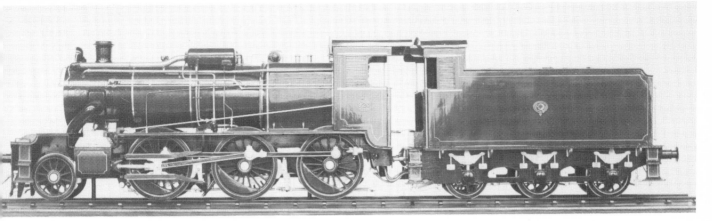

Egypt. At the Empire Exhibition held in Glasgow in 1938 this fine scale-model locomotive was on display on the stand of the North British Locomotive Co. It was a small replica of 2-6-0 No. 920 of the Egyptian State Railways, of a type of which the company had constructed 20 in that year. These Egyptian engines were designed for mixed traffic working on lines restricted to light axle-loads. They were equipped with Caprotti valve gear and ACFI feed-water heaters. Their cylinders were 17¾in. × 28in. and the coupled wheels 5ft 6¾in. The boiler-barrel was slightly tapered, its working-pressure being 225lb./in.². The grate-area was 25 sq. ft. Including the 24-element Melesco superheater, the total heating-surface was 1,696 sq. ft. The tractive effort at 85 per cent of boiler-pressure was 25,267 lb.

Locomotive and tender weighed 107¾ tons in working order, the latter being provided with roller bearing axle-boxes and holding 3,700 gallons of water and six tons of coal. The finish was bright green with black bands lined white, and the tender bore the ESR emblem consisting of a garter enclosing a crescent moon and three stars.
Photo: Mitchell Library, Glasgow

Britain. The high degree of realism achieved by this superb model **(overleaf)** of London Midland & Scottish Pacific No. 6230 *Duchess of Buccleuch* is quite extraordinary. Only in the matter of size does it differ from its prototype. H. C. Powell, onetime Works Foreman at Crewe, where its namesake was built, completed the model to ⅛th scale in 1948. It is fully operational, embodies four working cylinders and is coal-fired. It made its public *debut* in London at the *Model Engineer* Exhibition of 1948, at which F. C. Hambleton, J. N. Maskelyne, both well known in the model railway world, and the author formed the judging committee for locomotive and railway models. One recalls what a comparatively easy task it was with such a model in the field for an award. It was a comfortable winner of the locomotive championship cup. At the time of writing this outstanding model locomotive may be seen in the Science Museum, South Kensington, on loan from Col. R. J. Hoare.

Its prototype, and four others named after duchesses, were completed in 1938 to the design of W. A. (later Sir William) Stanier, the LMS Chief Mechanical Engineer. They were a non-streamlined (and much better looking) version of the class 7P *Coronation* Pacifics, of which 24 were built. Their four cylinders were 16¼in. × 28in., coupled wheels 6ft 9in. and boiler-pressure 250lb./in.², at 85 per cent of which the tractive power was 40,000lb. Total evaporative heating-surface was 2,807½ sq. ft, supplemented by the superheater-surface of 856 sq. ft, and there was 50 sq. ft of grate-area. Operational weight of engine and tender, which held 4,000 gallons of water and 10 tons of coal, was 161¾ tons. The *Duchesses* became the standard heavy express-passenger locomotives of the LMS; the casing from their streamlined sisters was eventually removed to facilitate servicing, and never restored.
Photo: Science Museum, South Kensington

U.S.A. Steam-locomotives having the 4-8-4 or Northern wheel-arrangement were among the best ever to be employed for mixed-traffic service in the United States. Baldwin built 12 of this type in 1938 for the Atlantic Coast Line Railroad. Known as class R–1, they were given two cylinders 27in. × 30in., coupled wheels 6ft 8in. and a boiler working-pressure of 275lb./in.². The grate-area was $97\frac{7}{10}$ sq. ft and the total evaporative heating-surface 4,753 sq. ft. They scaled 447 tons and had a tractive effort of 63,900lb. Their 16-wheeled tenders held 27 tons of coal, which were fed to the firebox by mechanical stoker, and 24,000 gallons of water.

When used for the winter tourist traffic between Richmond, Virginia, and Jacksonville, Florida, these 4-8-4s demonstrated that they could handle trains of up to 20 cars at an average speed of 64 mph. The model of No. 1805, which is to be seen in the Smithsonian Institution, was made by Bassett-Lowke Ltd to a scale of $\frac{1}{2}$in. to 1ft.
Photo: Smithsonian Institution, Washington

Canada. In 1939 King George VI and Queen Elizabeth travelled 8,377 miles by rail in Canada and the United States, chiefly over the metals of the Canadian National and Canadian Pacific Railways. Their special train was given a royal blue livery which was also worn by the Canadian locomotives entrusted with its haulage. The Canadian Pacific used one engine throughout its part of the tour, the semi-streamlined 4-6-4 No. 2850, which had been built in 1938. Of impressive design, it weighed 334 tons in working order with its 12-wheeled tender. Its grate-area measured 80⅘ sq. ft and it had a total heating-surface of 5,501 sq ft. Cylinders 22in. × 30in., coupled wheels 6ft 3in. and a boiler-pressure of 275 lb./in.² produced a tractive effort of 45,000lb.

In 1940 Jack Hewitson built the ¾in. to 1ft working scale-model of No. 2850 illustrated. It has an overall length of 6ft and weighs 140 lb. The boiler-pressure is 90lb./in.² and its equipment includes superheater and mechanical lubricator. The striking royal blue livery of the prototype was faithfully reproduced, save that the royal coat of arms was centred on the tender instead of being positioned nearer the leading end. This was done because the model was displayed, without a train, at the New York World Fair in 1940, at the request of the Canadian Pacific.
Photo: Jack Hewitson

Germany. Steam-power on the Deutsche Reichsbahn was considerably strengthened by the advent of the class 50 two-cylinder 2-10-0 freight locomotives in 1939. They are represented in the Verkehrsmuseum at Nürnberg by the well-finished ⅛th scale-model of the pioneer engine No. 50.001.

Their cylinders were 23⅝in. × 26in., as in the case of the class O1 engines, and the coupled wheels 4ft 7$\frac{1}{10}$in. With a working-pressure of 235lb./in.² the tractive power was 59,424lb. Total heating-surface was 2,765 sq. ft, with a grate-area of 42 sq. ft. In working order, engine and tender weighed 146$\frac{3}{10}$ tons. All German locomotive-builders took part in the construction of more than 3,000 of these engines over the years 1939–1942.
Photo: Verkehrsmuseum, Nürnberg

East Africa. Beyer-Garratt locomotives proved their worth on the onerous metre-gauge main line of the Kenya & Uganda Railways, which extended from Mombasa to Kampala, a distance of 879 miles. In 1939, thirty-six 4-8-2+2-8-4s were working passenger and freight services. In that year six 4-8-4+4-8-4s were delivered by Beyer Peacock & Co. They had 4ft 6in. coupled wheels, four cylinders 16in. × 26in., a working-pressure of 220lb./in.² and a tractive effort of 46,090lb. The boilers were then regarded as exceptionally large for the metre-gauge, being of 6ft 6¼in. diameter. The total heating-surface, tubes, firebox and superheater was 2,750 sq. ft and there was 48½ sq. ft of grate-area. Nicholson thermic syphons were provided. With a full load of 6,000 gallons of water and 12 tons of coal the operational weight amounted to 186 tons 6 cwt.

These engines eventually became 57th class of the East African Railways, which were formed in 1948 by the amalgamation of the Kenya & Uganda and Tanganyika Railways. One of them, No. 5701, was modelled to a scale of ¾in. to 7ft by Bassett-Lowke Ltd for Beyer Peacock and Co. in 1950. It is shown in EAR livery in the accompanying photograph.
Photo: Bassett-Lowke Ltd

Britain. The 2-8-0Ts of the Great Western first appeared in 1910 and were designed for the movement of heavy coal-traffic in South Wales. As originally built the cylinders were 18½in. × 30in. (later 19in. × 30in.) and the coupled wheels 4ft 7½in. The heating-surface, including that of the superheater-tubes, was 1,566¾ sq. ft (later 1,670¼ sq. ft) and the grate-area 20½ sq. ft. The boiler-pressure was 200lb./in.². In their final form these engines weighed just over 82 tons in working order (including 1,800 gallons of water and three tons of coal) and possessed a tractive effort of 33,170lb.

All the characteristics of the design have been captured in F. Cottam's splendid 5in. gauge working model of No. 5255 of the final batch of 1940. The copper-brazed boiler was hydraulically tested to 200lb./in.² and steam-tested to 180 lb. for a working-pressure of 75 lb. The boiler-feed includes two injectors and axle-driven pump. The wheels are of cast-iron having coupled axles with ball-bearing axle-boxes and laminated springs of phosphor-bronze. Cylinders are lubricated by a sight-feed lubricator, with an oil reservoir under the cab floor. Automatic vacuum and handbrakes are fitted and there is a combined ejector and brake in the cab, the air-pump driven from the righthand crosshead. The model took 15 years to build and was completed in 1967. It deservedly won a silver medal at the *Model Engineer* Exhibition 1968 and is now the property of Humphrey Platts of Grantham.
Photo: Alan Milner

New Zealand. The 145 ton class Ka 4-8-4 locomotives of the New Zealand Railways were constructed almost to the limits of the restricted loading gauge, which imposes a maximum height above rail of 11ft 6in. and a maximum width of 8ft 6in., and to the maximum permitted axle-load of 14 tons. They were designed for principal main line services in the North Island. 35 were completed at the NZR Hutt workshops over the years 1939–1950. From about 1946 onwards all were altered or built to burn fuel-oil, so as to eliminate manually coal-firing a grate-area of $47\frac{7}{10}$ sq. ft. Cylinders were 20in. × 26in., coupled wheels 4ft 6in. and the working pressure 200lb./in.² Roller-bearings were pro-

vided on all axles, including those of the tender.

Ka locomotives could haul a 1,000-ton freight train on the level and they were capable of a speed of 60–65 mph with trains of 400 tons. But by 1967 they had been replaced by diesel electric traction. Two of them have been saved for possible restoration and preservation. In the middle 1950s Frank Roberts made the $\frac{1}{2}$in. to 1ft scale-model illustrated of No. 931. It is, in fact, a rebuild of a class K 4-8-4 he supplied to the NZR for its Centennial Exhibition model railway and is powered with an electric-motor.
Photo: New Zealand Railways Publicity & Advertising Dept

Rhodesia. The first Beyer-Garratt locomotives to be operated on the 3ft 6in. gauge Rhodesia Railways were a dozen 2-6-2+2-6-2 engines received from Beyer Peacock & Co. Ltd. in 1926. Their task was to work the traffic over the difficult section between Vila Machado and Umtali, on which the ruling grade is 1 in 50 uncompensated with curves of 5 chains.

Since then Beyer-Garratt locomotives have been increasingly employed, one of the most successful types being the 15th class 4-6-4+4-6-4, the first batch of which was introduced in 1940 for hauling Cape Town and Johannesburg mail-trains between Bulawayo and Mafeking. This class has bar frames, 17½in. × 26in. cylinders, 4ft 9in. diameter coupled wheels, a tractive effort of 42,750lb. at 85 per cent working pressure and weigh 179½ tons in working order. The model of No. 272 illustrated was built by Bassett-Lowke Ltd in 1947, to a scale of ¾in. to 1ft, for Beyer Peacock & Co. Ltd.
Photo: Bassett-Lowke Ltd

India. This Bassett-Lowke model of a Beyer-Garratt 4-8-2+2-8-4 locomotive, No. 857 of the Bengal–Nagpur Railway, was made to a scale of 10mm. to 1ft in 1955. Its full-size prototype was one of a class of four built by Beyer Peacock & Co. Ltd in 1940 specially for working the Anuppur–Chirmiri coalfields line which, in its 54 miles, abounded in curves, some as tight as 716 and 570ft radius, a ruling gradient of 1 in 91 and a maximum permitted axle-load of 17 tons. The Bengal–Nagpur, now South Eastern Railway, is one of the broad-gauge Indian systems, being mainly constructed to a gauge of 5ft 6in.

The Beyer-Garratts, with 4ft 8in. coupled wheels, a fixed wheelbase of 10ft 4½in. and a tractive effort of 68,660lb replaced conventional 4-6-0 engines with 4ft 3in. coupled wheels, a fixed wheelbase of 10ft 11in. and a tractive effort of 22,500lb. Other principal dimensions of the Beyer-Garratts are four cylinders 20½in. × 26in., a total heating-surface of 4,114 sq. ft, a grate-area of 70 sq. ft, boiler-diameter of 7ft 0in., boiler-pressure of 210lb./in.², an overall length of 101ft 6in. and a weight in working order of 230 tons. As in the case of contemporary engines of this type, the valve-gear of the two power-units was coupled so as to bring the quadrant blocks into the same relative position.
Photo: Bassett–Lowke Ltd

Chile. This massive model is a $\frac{1}{10}$th reproduction of super-heated 4-8-2 No. 1105 of the Chilean State Railways. It was made in the model workshop of the central naval yard of San Bernardo in 1940.

Its prototype was constructed in the same year by the American Locomotive Co. for the southern lines of the system, which extended for some 1,780 miles on the 5ft 6in. gauge from Santiago and Valparaiso to Puerto Montt. With two 25in. × 30in. cylinders, 5ft 6in. coupled wheels and a 235lb. working-pressure the tractive effort is 56,750lb. The total evaporative heating surface is 3,648 sq. ft, the super-heating surface 1,118 sq. ft and the grate area $75\frac{2}{3}$ sq. ft. Engine and tender weigh 216 tons, the capacity of the latter being 8,982 US gallons of water and 11 US tons of coal.
Photo: Chilean State Railways

U.S.A. The class S62 B-B diesel-electric locomotives of the Chicago, Rock Island & Pacific are typical of numerous road switchers in the United States. They were built by American Locomotive Co. and General Electric Co. in 1941 and were powered by 1,000 hp six-cylinder-in-line turbo-supercharged four-cycle engines. They were carried on 3ft 4in. wheels and weighed 115 tons. In the Smithsonian Institution is displayed this model of No. 748 of the class. It was made to a scale of $\frac{1}{2}$in. to 1ft.
Photo: Smithsonian Institution, Washington

U.S.A. What an unforgettable sight the *Big Boys* of the Union Pacific must have presented when working hard with a heavy load up grade. The nickname was appropriate for they were among the biggest and most powerful steam-locomotives ever to be built. Overall, with their massive tenders, they measured 130ft 9¼in. in length, weighed 729 tons and possessed a tractive effort of 135,375 lb. The accompanying photograph of the ½in. to 1ft scale-model of No. 4000, the first of the class, made by Severn-Lamb Ltd for the Smithsonian Institution, conveys a good idea of the immensity of the design. Six feet in length and 9in. high, its construction took 3,000 man-hours.

Twenty of these 4-8-8-4 fast freight engines were built in 1941 by the American Locomotive Co. for the Union Pacific Railway. They were designed to operate unassisted, at speeds of up to 80 mph and over 1.14 per cent grades, between Ogden in Utah and Green River in Wyoming, across the Wahsatch mountains. Their four cylinders were 23¾in. × 32in., to which steam was distributed by 12in.

piston-valves actuated by Walschaerts gear controlled by power reversing gear. The diameter of the coupled wheels was 5ft 8in. and that of the leading and trailing truck wheels 3ft and 3ft 6in. respectively. The entire unit ran on roller-bearings.

The boiler supplied superheated steam at a pressure of 300lb./in.² Its evaporative heating-surface was made up of 593 sq. ft in the firebox and combustion-chamber, 111 sq. ft in the circulators and 5,185 sq. ft in the tubes and flues, making a total of 5,889 sq. ft, supplemented by 2,466 sq. ft superheater-area. The enormous grate was 150 3/10 sq. ft in area. Fourteen 3ft 6in. wheels carried the 194 ton tender, its capacity being 25,000 US gallons of water and 28 short tons of coal which, needless to say, was fed to the firebox by mechanical stoker.

Photos: Severn-Lamb Ltd

U.S.A. With a tractive effort of 50,000lb., the class P7 4-6-2s of the Baltimore & Ohio Railroad were the most powerful Pacifics yet built when they emerged from Baldwin Locomotive Works in 1927. Twenty were constructed for high-speed passenger-services and were named after the first 20 presidents of the United States. They were given a smart livery of olive green, lined golden yellow.

In 1935 the livery was changed to royal blue, unlined, and eight years later the names were removed. This plate reproduces a beautiful model of No. 5300, the first of the class, formerly *President Washington*, in its final condition. Made to a scale of ½in. to 1ft, it is to be seen in the B & O Transportation Museum in Baltimore. Its maker's name has not survived.

These engines had two cylinders 27in. × 28in. and coupled wheels 6ft 8in. The boiler-pressure was 230lb./in.², the evaporative heating-surface 3,846 sq. ft, including two thermic syphons, the superheater surface 932 sq. ft and the grate-area 70$\frac{3}{16}$ sq. ft. The tenders held 17½ tons of coal and 11,000 gallons of water and were fitted with water pick-up gear. Engine and tender weighed 270 tons in working order.

With a load of twelve passenger cars weighing 942 tons, the 226-mile run between Washington and New York (Jersey City) was performed in 4¾ hours, inclusive of eight intermediate stops.

Photo: B & O Transportation Museum, Baltimore

PLATE XI

U.S.A. This perfect $\frac{1}{16}$th scale replica of a class Ps-4 Pacific locomotive of the Southern Railway of the United States must be unique. The manufacture of its multifarious components was shared by ten scattered workshops of the railway company and when the model was erected at the Finley shops in Birmingham, Alabama during 1931, all the parts fitted with precision and without recourse to any alterations. Although the locomotive is equipped with a small electric motor, it is a working model in the true sense of the word. The Westinghouse cross-compound air pump, carved out of a solid block of brass, will function satisfactorily under a pressure of 55lb. The feed-water heater-pump, the engine of the standard type B mechanical stoker, the air-operated butterfly fire-doors, the turbogenerator and the pneumatic bellringer all work correctly. The cab has sliding windows and is lined with mahogany. The double-bogie tender, made up of 2,600 components, has 1,300 rivets in its cistern.

There were altogether 62 class Ps-4 Pacifics, their design derived from the USRA 4-6-2 of World War I, and they were constructed for the Southern by the American Locomotive Co. and Baldwins between 1923 and 1928. Their duties included the haulage of the *Crescent*, *Piedmont*, *Royal Palm* and *Ponce de Leon* expresses. Their livery of green, lined gold, was a refreshing change from the sombre garb of most American locomotives.

The leading dimensions of the prototype and the model make an interesting comparison:

	Ps-4 No. 1409	Model No. 1410
Dia. of cylinders	27in.	1.687in.
Stroke of cylinders	28in.	1.750in.
Dia. of coupled wheels	73in.	4.562in.
Working-pressure	200lb.	200lb.
Heating-surface	3174sq. ft	535sq. in.
Grate-area	70⅓sq. ft	36⅓sq. in.
Tractive effort	47,500lb.	185.68lb.

Taken in hand at a time of trade depression, the model must have been something of a morale-builder among the staff. It is certainly an outstanding example of enlightened management and employee teamwork and, appropriately, it has been given a place in the boardroom of the Southern in Washington DC.

Photo: Southern Railway Company

PLATE XII

Japan. A $\frac{1}{12}$th scale-model of 2-Co+Co-2 express passenger electric locomotive No. 8000 of the 3ft 6in. gauge Japanese Government Railways (now known as the Japanese National Railways), which is to be seen in the Museum of Transport, Glasgow. Its maker is not known.

The 1,830hp prototype was one of a number built by the North British Locomotive Co. and English Electric Co. in 1935 for an overhead-line, 1,500-volt DC system. It was carried on 4ft 7⅜in. driving-wheels, actuated by six traction-motors, and 3ft 1in. bogie wheels. The total wheelbase was 60ft 3in. and the length over buffers 69ft 7in. In working order the weight was 98¾ tons, of which 72 tons were available for adhesion. These locomotives hauled expresses up to 60 mph over the Tokyo-Yokohama-Kobe trunk line.
Photo: Museum of Transport, Glasgow

PLATE XIII

Britain. On 3 July 1938 No. 4468 *Mallard*, one of Gresley's incomparable class A4 streamlined Pacifics, steamed north from London for Grantham, ostensibly to continue brake trials being carried out that summer with a set of the *Coronation* express coaches. This time, however, the dynamometer car was in the make-up, the total tare weight of the train being 236½ tons. On the return from Grantham a successful attempt was made upon the world's speed record. Using full regulator with a 40 per cent cut-off, driver Duddington accelerated to 74½ mph in six miles up a continuous rising gradient of 1 in 198. Then over Stoke summit 116 mph was attained within six miles, followed by a momentary peak of 126 mph at milepost 90¼ from London. That record for steam-traction is now unlikely ever to be approached or surpassed. During World War II the A4s showed that they had great reserves of power as well as speed. On one occasion *Mallard* recovered eight minutes' lost time from Newcastle to Grantham with the *Flying Scotsman* made up to 710 tons.

Thirty-five A4s were built by the London & North Eastern Railway, the original livery of silver grey being eventually replaced by one of Garter blue, with crimson red wheels. Their three cylinders were 18½in. × 26in., steam-distribution being effected by Gresley's conjugated valve-gear with two sets of Walschaerts gear. Coupled wheels were 6ft 8in. and the boiler-pressure 250lb./in.², at 85 per cent of which the tractive power was 35,455lb. Total heating-surface (including superheater) and grate-area were 3,255 and 41½ sq. ft respectively and the operational weight of engine and tender was 167½ tons. *Mallard* and three companions built in 1938 differed from the earlier engines in that they were fitted with Kylchap double chimneys and twin blast-pipes.

This beautiful ¾in. to 1ft scale-model of *Mallard* is to be seen at York. Normally kept in Hudson House, the railway administrative offices, it has temporarily become part of the *décor* of the *Railway Mania*, a new bar in the Royal Station Hotel. It is a non-working model completed in December 1962 for British Railways by H. Clarkson & Son, and is a superb example of craftsmanship, being perfect in every external detail. The No. 60022 was assigned to the prototype by British Railways. The livery is a reproduction of the mundane green eventually adopted for some classes of express locomotives and worn by the A4s at the time of their withdrawal from service.
Photo: British Railways

PLATE XIV

France. This well-finished model, owned by G. P. Keen, portrays in 7mm. to 1ft scale the class 141R 2-8-2 mixed-traffic locomotive of the French Railways (SNCF). It is electrically operated, picking up current with the collectors which can be seen fore and aft of the tender-bogies, and will traverse a curve of 4ft 6in. radius. It has a boat-type motor in the tender, the drive being transmitted to the coupled wheels by cable and universal joint. 700 class 141R locomotives were put in hand by the American Locomotive Co., the Baldwin Locomotive Works and the Lima Locomotive Co. in 1944. This was done under contracts awarded by the French Provisional Government, which was faced with the destruction of more than 90 per cent of the locomotive-stock during the war. The model represents one of the Lima-built engines.

Their boilers carried a pressure of 220lb./in.² They were fitted with completely welded fireboxes, which had a grate-area of 55½ sq. ft extending into a 40in. long combustion-chamber, the heating-surface of the whole being 231 sq. ft. A further 63 sq. ft was provided by two firebox syphons and 704 sq. ft was contributed by the superheater. The heating-surface of the boiler-tubes and flues amounted to 2,405 sq. ft.

Fittings included a mechanical stoker. With 23½in. × 28in. outside cylinders of cast-steel and 5ft 3in. coupled wheels the tractive effort was 44,500lb. at 85 per cent of the boiler-pressure. Total weight of engine and tender in working order was 186 tons, the capacity of the latter being 8,070 gallons of water and a little less than 11¼ tons of coal.
Photo: G. P. Keen

Canada. A fine ¾in. to 1ft working scale-model of Canadian Pacific 4-6-2 No. 1201, built by Jack Hewitson in 1961 and displayed at the Union station in Ottawa. Its boiler has a working pressure of 90lb./in.² and its equipment includes piston-valves, superheater and mechanical lubricator. Its overall length is 4ft 8½in. and weight in working order 125 lb.

In contrast, the prototype, which was built in 1944, had a working-pressure of 250lb./in.², measured 76ft 4in. in overall length and weighed 203 tons in working order. Its cylinders were 20in. × 28in. and coupled wheels 6ft 8in. No. 1201 was one of a class destined to be the last Canadian Pacific steam-locomotive design for all purposes, freight and passenger.
Photo: James Sandilands

U.S.A. This impressive working model of Union Pacific 4-8-4 No. 835 is displayed in the Ontario Science Centre at Don Mills, Ontario. It was built to a scale of $\frac{3}{4}$in. to 1ft by A. Roedding of Toronto and was the result of 10,000 hours' work.

Its prototype was a veritable giant among non-articulated steam-locomotives. The two cylinders were 25in. × 32in., the coupled wheels 6ft 8in. and the boiler-pressure 300lb./in.², producing a tractive effort of 63,800 lb. Total evaporative heating-surface ran to 4,294 sq. ft, of which the firebox accounted for 442 sq. ft. The superheater-surface was 1,400 sq. ft and the grate-area a little over 100 sq. ft. The engine was oil-fired and its 14-wheeled tender carried 25 tons of oil fuel and 23,500 US gallons of water. Total operational weight of locomotive and tender amounted to nearly 403 tons. 45 were built for the Union Pacific by the American Locomotive Co. in 1944. The long smoke-deflector plates were a later addition.
Photo: Ontario Science Centre, Don Mills

Roumania. The standard 'austerity' general utility locomotive of the German State Railways during the last war was the class 52 2-10-0, of which about 5,000 were built, mostly by Henschel & Son of Cassel. Over 300 were allocated to Austria and 100 went to Roumania, some of the latter being constructed by Borsig. A splendid, fully detailed scale model of the Roumanian State Railways version, No. 150.001, is illustrated. It was made in the workshops of Grivita Rosie to $\frac{1}{10}$th scale and is displayed in the Budapest Museum of Communication.

The full-size locomotive was given 23$\frac{3}{8}$in. × 26in. cylinders, 4ft 7$\frac{1}{10}$in. coupled wheels and a working-pressure of 227lb./in.² The total evaporative heating-surface was 2,038$\frac{3}{8}$ sq. ft, the superheater surface 685$\frac{1}{2}$ sq. ft and the grate-area 42 sq. ft. The engine weighed 84$\frac{2}{8}$ tons, with 75$\frac{3}{10}$ tons adhesive, and the double-bogie tender, which held eight tons of coal and 5,725 gallons of water scaled 59$\frac{3}{10}$ tons in working order. Additional locomotives of this class were built in the Reshita works of Roumania during the years 1946–1950.
Photo: Museum of Communication, Budapest

U.S.A. The Shay locomotive was the brainchild of Ephraim Shay, an ingenious lumberman who saw in it a means of securing flexibility of movement, albeit at low speeds, over rough, hilly and sharply curved track, together with a high power and weight ratio. It departs from conventional steam-locomotive design in that all axles of its supporting bogie trucks are gear driven from a horizontal shaft outside the wheels on the right-hand side of the engine. This shaft is a continuation of the crankshaft driven by vertical cylinders in line on the side of the boiler, which is offset several inches to the left of the centre of the track. Lima Locomotive Works built their last Shay, a B-B-B, in 1945. It was ordered by the standard-gauge Western Maryland Railroad, on which it became No. 6. Its three cylinders were 17in. × 18in. and its 12 wheels 4ft, each bogie-truck having a wheelbase of 5ft 4in. The working-pressure was 200lb./in.², the grate-area 48½ sq. ft and the total evaporative heating-surface 1,849 sq. ft with a superheating surface of 429 sq. ft. The coal and water capacities were nine tons and 6,000 US gallons respectively. In working order the unit weighed 144½ tons and possessed a tractive effort of 59,740 lb.

Models of Shay locomotives are extremely rare. The example illustrated differs from its Western Maryland prototype only because the trailing bogie-truck, carrying the water-tank, was omitted. This was done to make driving easier, for the model is a working one. Thus the coal bunker acts as water-tank and the car on which the driver sits behind the locomotive carries the coal. The model was built by the late Eric Coleby, an officer of the London & North Eastern Railway. Its scale is ¾in. to 1ft and it runs on 3½in. gauge track. The superheated copper boiler has a working-pressure of 100lb./in.² and a very deep firebox, 3in. at the throat plate, which permits the combustion of any old coal, from dust to anthracite, to produce ample steam. The three cylinders are of cast-iron with slide valves (the prototype had piston-valves) and the three sets of Stephenson valve-gear have launch-type links. Drive to the bogies is through universal joints, slightly different from those of Lima pattern, and the gear ratio is 5:3 (slightly higher than that of the prototype) actuating all axles. The bogies follow the full-size version, having spring-suspension on the left-hand side only. Water-feed is by injector or duplex pump in front of the engine-unit. The oil-pump is gear-driven off the crank-shaft with a 40:1 reduction. With a full head of steam the model Shay can move half a ton.

Photo: Richard Coleby

Britain. The *West Country* Pacifics of the Southern Railway, introduced in 1945 and respresented here by the $\frac{1}{16}$th scale-model of No. 21C102 *Salisbury* in the Science Museum, was a somewhat smaller version of O. V. Bulleid's well-known *Merchant Navy* class. They were designed to provide motive-power which could be used on the restricted and difficult routes west of Exeter. By extensive welding, the route availability achieved with the *West Country* engines was 90 per cent of the Southern system.

With three cylinders 16$\frac{3}{8}$in. × 24in., coupled wheels 6ft 2in. and a working-pressure of 280lb./in.² a tractive effort of 31,000lb was obtained. The total heating-surface was 2,667 sq. ft, of which the superheater accounted for 545 sq. ft, while the grate area was 38$\frac{1}{4}$ sq. ft. The weight on each coupled axle was 18$\frac{3}{4}$ tons, as compared with 21 tons of the *Merchant Navy* class. Weight of engine and tender in working order was 128$\frac{3}{8}$ tons, which included five tons of coal and 4,500 gallons of water in the tender. Features of the *Merchant Navy* locomotives, such as clasp brakes, BFB wheel-centres, Bulleid valve-gear, thermic syphons and 'air-smoothed' casing, were embodied; the livery was malachite green with yellow lettering, numbering and lining.
Photo: Science Museum, London

U.S.S.R. After World War II an entirely new 2-10-0 freight locomotive was designed for the USSR Railways. Its maximum permissible axle-load was set at 18 tons, so that it could enjoy a wide range of operation over the then devastated system, yet its power output had to approach that of the heavier class FD 2-10-2. In addition, it had to be amenable to mass production. These considerations were fulfilled by the class L 2-10-0, so designated after the name of its chief designer, L. S. Lebedianski. The first were built at Kolomna works in 1945 and were an immediate success. Several thousand have since been constructed.

The design embodied bar, instead of plate frames, and of its 103 tons operational-weight, 91 tons are available for adhesion. The coupled wheels are 4ft 11in., the two cylinders $24\frac{3}{8}$in. × $31\frac{1}{2}$in. and the boiler-pressure 206lb./in.². The heating-surface amounts to $2,389\frac{1}{2}$ sq. ft, the superheater-surface to 1,227 sq. ft and the grate-area to $64\frac{1}{2}$ sq. ft. The designed speed was 80 kmph. In the USSR Railways Museum the class is represented by this $\frac{1}{20}$th scale-model of No. 0005.
Photo: USSR Railways

South Africa. The class SI 0-8-0 shunting locomotives of the South African Railways were introduced in 1947 and were an enlargement of the class S 0-8-0 of 1929. The first dozen were built in the SAR workshops at Salt River and were given Nos. 374–385. No. 375 is the subject of the model illustrated, which was made by the META consortium in 1951–1952 to a scale of 7mm. to 1ft and is now in the Railway Museum, Johannesburg.

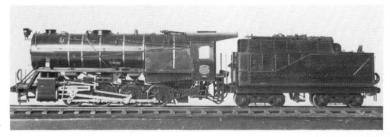

These engines can handle 2,000 tons. They have $23\frac{1}{4}$in. × 25in. cylinders and 4ft coupled wheels which, with a boiler-pressure of 180lb./in.², create a tractive effort of 38,000lb. The total heating-surface is 1,820 sq. ft, the superheater-area 428 sq. ft and the grate-area 42 sq. ft. With 11 tons of coal and 6,000 gallons in the bogie tender the total weight in working order is just over 140 tons.
Photo: SAR Publicity & Travel Department

Switzerland. Brown Boveri of Baden made this $\frac{1}{10}$th-scale-model of Rhaetian Railway class Ge4/4 Bo-Bo electric-locomotive No. 601 in 1947. It is displayed in the Swiss Transport Museum. Its prototype was built in the same year by Swiss Locomotive & Machine Works, Brown Boveri and Oerlikon. It was the first of a batch of ten which demonstrated their ability to haul loads of 180 tons at 46 kmph over a sharply curved metre-gauge track beset with 35 per cent gradients.

These 1,600 hp locomotives weigh 46 tons. Their maximum speed is 75 kmph, the wheel diameter being 3ft 6in. With separately motorised axles the general design is very similar to the Bern-Lötschberg-Simplon class Ae 4/4¹ engines, which were the first express locomotives to dispense altogether with idle carrying-axles.
Photo: Swiss Transport Museum, Lucerne

France. French craftsmanship at its best is exemplified by this beautifully finished reproduction of 242.A.1 of the SNCF. It was made by Jean Lequesne of Dieppe to a scale of 7mm. to 1ft, 1¼in. gauge, and is complete in all external details. The prototype was a famous rebuild of the illustrious engineer André Chapelon, whose influence was felt throughout Europe and who was remarkable in that so many of his finest achievements in raising locomotive efficiency were carried out on the designs of others.

In this case the original locomotive was one of a series of 4-8-2s constructed by the Compagnie de Fives-Lille in 1932 for the French State Railways (Chemin de Fer de l'Etat). It was a three-cylinder simple expansion machine. Chapelon, who was an ardent exponent of compounding, transformed it into a three-cylinder 4-8-4. The extra pair of wheels under the firebox was required because the strengthening of the frame increased the engine weight by 20 tons to 148 tons. The inner 23⅜in. × 28³/₁₀in. high-pressure cylinder drove the leading pair of coupled wheels and the two outside 26⅘in. × 29⁹/₁₀in. low-pressure cylinders the second pair. Walschaerts gear distributed steam by Trick valves to the high-pressure cylinder and by Willoteaux valves to the low-pressure cylinders. Coupled wheels were 6ft 4½in.

Two Nicholson thermic syphons with a heating-surface of 67⅕ sq. ft were built into the steel firebox, which had a heating-surface of 268 sq. ft, bringing the total evaporative heating-surface to 2,720 sq. ft. The grate-area, fed by a Hudson mechanical stoker, amounted to 53⅘ sq. ft. The Houlet superheater had a heating-surface of 1,294 sq. ft, the superheater temperature being 425°C. Because of the size of the boiler a triple Kylchap blast-pipe was fitted. During trial runs 242.A.1 developed a maximum of 4,200 hp at 56 mph on a gradient of 11 in 1,000 with a load of 611 tons. On acceleration tests 62 mph was reached with a train of 604 tons in 3 minutes 10 seconds.

Photo: Jean Lequesne

South Africa. Designed for operation on 45lb. rails, the class 24 branch-line locomotive was introduced to the South African Railways in 1948 by the Chief Mechanical Engineer Dr M. M. Loubser. They were the first examples in South Africa of the 2-8-4, or Berkshire, wheel-arrangement and also the first to have a cast-steel bed in which the cylinders and hind covers were cast integral with the frame-sides and stretchers. 100 were built by the North British Locomotive Co. and were allotted Nos. 3601–3700. They had 19in. × 26 in. cylinders and 4ft 3in. coupled wheels. The working-pressure was 200lb./in.², at 75 per cent of which the tractive effort was 27,600 lb. The heating-surface totalled 1,636 sq. ft and the superheater and grate areas were 380 sq. ft 36 sq. ft respectively.

A Vanderbilt tender, a little smaller in capacity than those which appeared on the class 19D 4-8-2 engines of 1949, was also an innovation for South Africa. Its capacity was 4,500 gallons of water and nine tons of coal, making the operational weight of the locomotive and tender just under 130 tons. The 7mm. to 1ft scale-model of No. 3607 in the Railway Museum at Johannesburg is reproduced. It was made in 1951–1952 by the META consortium.
Photo: SAR Publicity & Travel Department

South Africa. Sinclair Model Engineering Co. of Glasgow made this magnificent $\frac{1}{12}$th scale-replica of class 15F 4-8-2 No. 3057 of the South African Railways. The full-size locomotive was the first of a batch of 100 built in 1948 by the North British Locomotive Co., becoming Nos. 3057–3156. The cylinders were 24in. × 28in., the coupled wheels 5ft and, with a boiler-pressure of 210lb./in.², the tractive effort (at 75 per cent boiler-pressure) was 42,340lb. The total heating-surface was 3,400 sq. ft, the superheater-area being 676 sq. ft and the grate-area 63 sq. ft. A mechanical stoker was provided. A double bogie tender holding 5,620 gallons of water and 14 tons of coal brought the total weight in working order up to 182 tons 14 cwt.
Photo: Mitchell Library, Glasgow

U.S.A. The most famous locomotives of the New York, Chicago & St Louis Railroad—better known as the Nickel Plate Road—are probably its class S2 2-8-4s or Berkshires, which originated in 1934. The superb model illustrated, to be seen in the Smithsonian Institution, was made to a scale of ½in. to 1ft. It is of No. 779, constructed by Lima Locomotive Works in 1949, and one of the last steam-locomotives to be turned out in the United States by a commercial builder. A large boiler and firebox which generated ample steam for the two 25in. × 34in. cylinders was an important feature of the design. Coupled wheels were 5ft 9in. and the boiler-pressure 245lb./in.². The engine possessed a tractive effort of 64,100 lb. and moved on roller-bearings. With its 12-wheeled tender it weighed 367 tons in working order.
Photo: Smithsonian Institution, Washington

Egypt. Twelve massive, green-bodied, yellow-lined, diesel-electric locomotives which appeared at the head of Egyptian State Railways Cairo-Port Said expresses in 1949 were in some respects similar to No. 10000, the first main line diesel locomotive of the London Midland & Scottish Railway. The chief affinity was the power-unit, a 16-cylinder V type 4 cycle turbo-charged engine, with a rating of 1,600 hp. The oil-engines and electrical gear were constructed by the English Electric Co., who were the main contractors. The mechanical part was designed by the English Electric Co. and the Vulcan Foundry Ltd, the latter providing the detailed design of the running gear and main frame. Six locomotives were erected in each company's works.

To conform to an axle-load of 17 tons, the rather unusual 1A-Do-A1 wheel-arrangement was adopted with a 16ft rigid wheelbase of four-motored axles at the centre and a bogie at each extremity, the inner axles of which were also motored. The driving wheels are 3ft 9in. diameter and the bogie-wheels 3ft. In working order the weight is 124 tons, of which 97½ tons are available for adhesion, and the maximum tractive effort 36,000 lb. The track gauge is the standard 4ft 8½in. The model illustrated was made to a scale of ½in. to 1ft for English Electric for publicity purposes. It is complete in all external details.
Photo: GEC Traction Ltd

Brazil. Overhead-line electrification at 3,000 volts DC of the onerous 40 miles section of the 5ft 3in. gauge Estrada de Ferro Santos a Jundiai (formerly Sao Paulo Railway) between Jundiai and the freight-yards at Mooca, near Sao Paulo, was inaugurated on 20 July 1950. A large proportion of the world's coffee is moved over the line, with its long Taipas and Belem banks at 1 in 40/50. To operate it, fifteen 3,000 hp mixed-traffic Co-Co locomotives were ordered from English Electric . . . a case of Co-Cos for coffee.

Vulcan Foundry designed and built the mechanical parts and erected the locomotives. Their length over buffers is 67ft 3in. and overall width 10ft 1in., the weight being 125 tons 3 cwt. The wheel-diameter is 4ft and all axleboxes are fitted with Timken roller-bearings. Six nose-suspended traction-motors are embodied and drive their respective axles through single-reduction gearing. Straight air-brakes, regenerative braking, vacuum-brake gear and hand-brakes are provided. The maximum permissible speed is 60 mph. The 10mm. to 1ft scale publicity model of locomotive No. 1001 was made by City Display Organisation for English Electric in 1950. It was given the maroon finish and silver band of the prototype.

Photo: GEC Traction Ltd

Holland. The appearance of electric-locomotives in Holland was delayed by the war and the first to go into service was the borrowed Bo+Bo locomotive No. 6701 of the London & North Eastern Railway, referred to on page 160. The first three of a batch of ten 1-Do-1 made their *début* in 1948 and two years later an order was placed for fifty 1,500 volt DC Bo-Bo locomotives from the French firm of Alsthom in Belfort.

These were numbered 1100 upwards and were very similar to the series BB 8100 of the French Railways. The $\frac{1}{10}$th scale-model illustrated of No. 1108 is to be seen in the Railway Museum, Utrecht. It was made in the main repair-shop of the Netherlands Railways in Haarlem in 1953. The class 1100 locomotives have 1,250mm. diameter wheels, a maximum tractive effort of 15,000 kg and a maximum speed of 135 kmph. They weigh 80 metric tons and have a pleasingly symmetrical appearance.
Photo: Railway Museum, Utrecht

Hungary. The 4-6-4s of series 303 were the biggest non-articulated steam locomotives to be operated by the Hungarian State Railways and the last express steam design to be built for the system. The first went into service in 1950. They were immense engines, with the top of their chimneys towering 15ft 3in. above rail-level. A splendid working model of one of these locomotives, made to $\frac{1}{10}$th scale, is included in the collection owned by Dr Alex Varga. It was constructed by him over the years 1964–1966. It is noteworthy as having been copied by the designer of the 40f value in the latest series of postage stamps issued by Hungary in 1972 to honour its railways, a graceful gesture which the British Post Office, to its shame, seems to be incapable of emulating.

The full-size series 303 locomotives were given $21\frac{2}{3}$in. × 26in. cylinders, 6ft $6\frac{3}{4}$in. coupled wheels and a working-pressure of 256lb./in.², which produced a tractive effort of 25,760lb. The total evaporative heating-surface was 2,583 sq. ft and the grate-area of $59\frac{1}{5}$ sq. ft was fed by a mechanical stoker. The engine had an operational weight of $107\frac{7}{10}$ tons, of which $53\frac{3}{10}$ tons rested on the coupled wheels. Rather unusually, the tender was carried on five axles, made up of four-wheeled leading and six-wheeled trailing bogies. Its capacity was 5,500 gallons of water and $12\frac{7}{10}$ tons of coal.
Photo: Dr Alex Varga

Britain. British Railways' first standard locomotive was the class 7 Pacific No. 70000 *Britannia*, which emerged from Crewe works early in 1951 to the designs of R. A. Riddles. It formed part of a batch of 25, the fifth of which, No. 70004 *William Shakespeare*, was exhibited at the Festival of Britain of that year. C. M. Amsbury of Kings Newton made this fine 3½in. gauge working model of *William Shakespeare*, based upon official drawings. It took five years to construct, being completed in 1966, and was awarded a silver medal and the Crebbin Memorial Trophy at the *Model Engineer* Exhibition of 1968. Its equipment includes correctly working twin water-gauges, reverser with indicator-dial, speedometer, steam-chest and boiler-pressure gauges and a complete vacuum brake system.

The full-size engine had two 20in. × 28in. cylinders, 6ft 2in. coupled wheels and a boiler pressure of 250lb./in.², the tractive effort being 32,160 lb. The heating-surface was made up of 2,264 sq. ft by the tubes and flues, 210 sq. ft by the firebox and 718 sq. ft by the superheater. The grate-area was 42 sq. ft. Measuring 68ft 9in. over buffers, the engine and tender were carried on Timken self-aligning roller-bearing axle-boxes and weighed 141 tons in working order. Water pick-up gear was provided on the tender, which had a welded tank of 4,250 gallons capacity. The coal bunker, narrower than the tank, held seven tons of coal.
Photo: C. M. Amsbury

New Zealand. In 1948 the first diesel-electric locomotives to operate on the New Zealand Railways were ordered from English Electric, which had already played a leading part in the supply of electric-locomotives and rolling stock since 1921. The prototype of the ½in. to 1ft scale-model illustrated, which was made by H. Clarkson & Son in 1954, was one of an order for ten 1,500 hp 2-Co-Co-2 main-line locomotives placed with English Electric in 1952. They were primarily for passenger and freight service on the North Island trunk line between Wellington and Auckland, 425 miles, the central portion of which is stiffly graded and sharply curved. There is, for example, one section of 1 in 60 for no less than 21 miles, including 14 miles at 1 in 50 with much 7½ chain curvature.

The locomotives can negotiate a 4½ chain curve. The wheel-diameter is 3ft 1in., the rigid wheelbase 12ft and the total wheelbase 52ft. Overall length over buffer-beams is 58ft and the overall width 8ft 4in. The engine is a four-stroke super-charged V-form unit with 12 cylinders 10in. × 12in. Three traction motors are mounted on each main bogie, and all bogies, main or pilot, are equipped with roller-bearing axleboxes of identical type. In working order the locomotives weigh 105 tons, with 69 tons adhesive, and are capable of a speed of 60 mph.

Photo: H. Clarkson & Son

Spain. In the early 1950's English Electric, in conjunction with Vulcan Foundry, built a fleet of 60 powerful Co-Co electric-locomotives for the 5ft 6in. gauge Red Nacional de los Ferrocarriles Espanoles, or RENFE for short, the Spanish National Railways. They were designed for passenger and freight train haulage on the Oviedo-Leon-Ponferrada 3,000 volt DC main line, the mountainous Ujo-Busdongo section of which has a practically continuous ruling gradient of 1 in 50. Several fine models of these locomotives, complete in all external details, have been produced, mainly for publicity purposes, by Westway Models, Shawcraft and City Display Organisation, the last-named having made the example illustrated. It is to ½in. to 1ft scale of No. 7701, finished in the blue-green of the prototype, with stainless-steel band and vermilion buffer-beams.

The first of the RENFE Co-Cos was completed in 1952. It will be seen that their design is very similar to that of the Santos-Jundiai locomotives on page 146. They were, in fact, 5½ tons lighter, despite a track-gauge 3in. wider, and 5¼in. longer overall. They were also more powerful, the six force-ventilated, axle-hung, nose-suspended traction-motors having a total one-hour rating of 3,600 hp. The braking arrangements were slightly different, but the wheel-diameter of 4ft was the same and other dimensions matched those of the Brazilian engines. Timken roller-bearings were fitted to the axleboxes of the first 20, the remainder having axleboxes of the Isothermos type.

Photo: GEC Traction Ltd

Greece. Good models of Greek locomotives seem to be great
rarities. The example illustrated is displayed in the Museo
Nazionale della Scienza e della Tecnica Leonardo da Vinci
in Milan, It was made by Ing. A. Siriati and reproduces,
in $\frac{1}{20}$th scale, one of the ten 2-8-2 metre-gauge locomotives
owned by the Piraeus-Athens-Peloponnesus Railway, which
became part of the Hellenic State Railways in 1962.

The oil-fired prototype was constructed by Breda of
Milan in 1952. The cylinders were 18½in. × 22in. and the
coupled wheels 3ft 11⅝in. The boiler, which had a working-
pressure of 155lb./in.², was given a heating-surface of
1,448¾ sq. ft, a superheater-surface of 376¾ sq. ft and a
grate-area of 29¾ sq. ft. The double-bogie tender carried
15 cu. metres of water and six cu. metres of fuel-oil. Operational weight of engine and tender was 95 tons and a curve of
262ft radius could be negotiated. As these locomotives
were designed to work at a maximum speed of 60 kmph,
the smoke-deflector plates were rather a luxury and were
subsequently removed.
*Photo: Museo Nazionale della Scienza è della Technica
Leonardo da Vinci, Milan*

Switzerland. In 1952 the first two class Ae 6/6 Co-Co locomotives of the Swiss Federal Railways, Nos. 11401 and 11402, appeared on the Gotthard line. They were designed for hauling 600 ton passenger trains at 40–46 mph up the long 1 in 37–40 banks on the lines from Lucerne or Zurich to Bellinzona and Chiasso, or freight trains of 750 tons over the same routes. These handsome 6,000 hp locomotives were built by the Swiss Locomotive Works, with electrical equipment by Brown Boveri. Their maximum starting effort is 72,800lb. and top speed 78 mph. Length over buffers is 60ft 5in. and the weight in working order 122 tons. The driving-bogies are set at 28ft 6in. centres and are carried on 4ft 1in. diameter wheels.

The Swiss Transport Museum model illustrated is one of the later locomotives named after cantons, No. 11412 *Zurich*. It was made to $\frac{1}{10}$th scale in the apprentices' workshop of the Swiss Federal Railways in Zurich.
Photo: Swiss Transport Museum, Lucerne

Australia. The 4ft 8½in. gauge New South Wales Government Railways placed an order in 1952 with Beyer Peacock & Co. Ltd for no less than 50 class AD-60 4-8-4+4-8-4 Beyer-Garratt locomotives. They were among the heaviest and most powerful ever to be constructed outside North America. In working order they weighed over 254¾ tons, measured 108ft 7in. over buffers and possessed a tractive effort of 59,560lb. at 85 per cent working-pressure on an axle load of 16 tons.

Their introduction obviated the re-laying of many miles of track and increased the capacity of the line. They were the first Beyer-Garratts to be fitted with cast-steel beds (of American manufacture), which each weighed some 13 tons and incorporated the cylinders and steam-chests. The four cylinders were 19¼in. × 26in. and the coupled wheels 4ft 7in. All the characteristics of these immense engines were captured in the model of No. 6002, built to a scale of 10mm. to 1ft by Bassett-Lowke Ltd in 1954. The finish is black with narrow red lining and red buffer-beams.
Photo: Bassett-Lowke Ltd

Brazil. Fourteen Bo-Bo 3,000 volt DC electric-locomotives were built by Metropolitan-Vickers in 1952 for the metre-gauge Rede Mineira de Viação in the Brazilian State of Minas Gerais. This railway, then newly electrified, is very undulating in character, with gradients as stiff as 3 per cent and curves of 100-metre radius. It is now part of the Central Eastern system of the National Railways.

They went into service between Divinopolis and Carlos Prates in 1953, and for handling trains down the long heavy grades were equipped with rheostatic brakes; these were designed to hold the train at a steady speed, leaving the air- and vacuum-brakes for use in emergency. Each all-welded bogie, carried on 3ft 7in. wheels, was provided with two axle-hung motors. The length of the locomotive over the Henricot type couplers was 39ft 6in. and the operational weight 49$\frac{1}{5}$ tons. The model illustrated of one of these locomotives was completed in 1951 by H. Clarkson & Son for Metropolitan-Vickers for the Festival of Britain. It was made to a scale of 10mm. to 1ft.
Photo: H. Clarkson & Son

Germany. With the end of World War II the German railway system was divided into two, Deutsche Bundesbahn (DB) of West Germany and Deutsche Reichsbahn (DR) of East Germany. The impressive model illustrated reproduces class 23 2-6-2 locomotive No. 23.001 of the DB, made to $\frac{1}{10}$th scale. It dominates the entrance-hall of the splendid Verkehrsmuseum in Nürnberg.

Class 23 was the first new passenger-engine design to appear in Western Germany since the outbreak of the war. Fifteen were completed in 1951 by Henschel, of which No. 23.001 was the first, followed by another ten by Arn. Jung in the same year. Their chief feature was an all-welded boiler that was totally devoid of rivets for seams, boiler-mounting seatings and brackets. The locomotive frame structure was also completely welded up as one piece.

Two $20\frac{1}{2}$in. $\times$ 26in. cylinders were embodied in the design. The coupled wheels were 5ft 9in. and the boiler-pressure 200lb./in.² Total evaporative heating-surface was 1,681 sq. ft, the superheater surface 794 sq. ft and the grate-area $33\frac{1}{2}$ sq. ft. The axle load was a moderate 17 tons, the total locomotive weight being about 80 tons. Operational weight of engine and tender, which had a length of 70ft over buffers, was 145 tons, including a full load of $7\frac{3}{4}$ tons of coal and 6,800 gallons of water. Maximum permissible speed was 110 kmph.
Photo: Verkehrsmuseum, Nürnberg

PLATE XV

Sudan. The GEC Traction collection of models for publicity display purposes contains this fine example of a 3ft 6in. gauge Sudan Railways diesel-electric locomotive made to a scale of ½in. to 1ft. It depicts one of 15 Co-Cos built by Vulcan Foundry in 1960 for working the heaviest passenger and goods trains on the system, including 1,500 ton cotton trains from Khartoum and the interior to Port Sudan on the Red Sea. It was constructed by Shawcraft Models.

These locomotives have to work under severe climatic conditions, which can embrace shade temperatures of 120°F, coupled with a relative humidity of 47 per cent, while the altitude reached by the line is 3,035ft above sea-level. Nevertheless, the English Electric 12CSVT engine will develop 1,850hp at 850 rpm by virtue of the inter-cooling equipment and specially matched pressure-chargers with which it is equipped. Dynamic and vacuum brakes are fitted to these locomotives, which weigh 99 tons in working order, are 55ft long and operate at a maximum speed of 45 mph.
Photo: GEC Traction Ltd

PLATE XVI

Australia. Here is an example of a model made before its prototype. This ¾in. to 1ft replica of New South Wales Government Railways Bo-Bo diesel-electric locomotive No. 4104 was completed by Bassett-Lowke Ltd in May 1952, to the order of British Thomson-Houston Ltd. The full-size 1,000 hp locomotive appeared the following year, the first of ten designed for the shunting and haulage of heavy freight-trains. It was very much a teamwork production. The design and layout was accomplished by BTH, who provided the electrical equipment, in collaboration with Metropolitan-Cammell Carriage & Wagon Co. Ltd, in whose Birmingham works the mechanical parts were manufactured and the locomotives assembled and tested. The diesel-engines were designed and made by Davey, Paxman & Co. Ltd.

The locomotives measure 43ft over buffer-beams, weigh some 80 tons and may be operated in multiple with control by one driver. All were in traffic by the end of March 1954, being based on Enfield depot and engaged almost entirely on freight-train duties in the Sydney area.

Photo: Bassett-Lowke Ltd

Australia. A fully detailed ½in. to 1ft scale-model of Queensland Railways Co-Co diesel-electric locomotive No. 1200, made in 1953 by H. Clarkson & Son for English Electric. The external finish is blue, with grey panels outlined in yellow at the leading end and trailing ends of the sides. Its 1,500 hp prototype is one of ten supplied by English Electric in the same year, the design and construction of the mechanical parts being the work of the Vulcan Foundry, who erected the locomotives at Newton-le-Willows. Each bogie, carried on 3ft 1½in. wheels, is fitted with three axle-hung, nose-suspended traction-motors and Timken roller-bearing axleboxes. The maximum axle-load is 15 tons, the maximum tractive effort 50,000lb. and the weight in working order 87½ tons.

These locomotives operate services on the 1,043 mile-long coastal line of the 3ft 6in. gauge Queensland Railways between Brisbane and Cairns, and between Brisbane and Toowoomba, including the *Sunlander* and *Inlander* air-conditioned expresses.

Photo: H. Clarkson & Son

U.S.A. In 1947 the Chesapeake & Ohio Railway bought 30 0-8-0 shunting locomotives which were sold to the Norfolk & Western Railway less than two years later. They were obviously thought more of by their new owner, for it built another 45 at its Roanoke shops between 1951 and 1953. One of them, No. 244, was destined to earn the distinction of becoming the last steam-locomotive to be built in North America. These engines had cylinders 24in. × 28in., coupled wheels 4ft 4in. in diameter and weighed, with their tenders, 230 tons in working order.

A ½in. scale-model of No. 201 of the class is illustrated. It was built by H. Clarkson & Son in 1969 and is to be seen in the Smithsonian Institution, Washington, DC.
Photo: H. Clarkson & Son

France. In the catalogue of model locomotives in the Museo Nazionale della Scienza e della Tecnica Leonardo da Vinci there is the laconic entry 'Locomotiva elettrica serie 9000 delle Ferrovie Francesi—anno. 1960.' What a cavalier way to treat a fine $\frac{1}{20}$th scale-reproduction of one of the two fastest locomotives in the world! For the model is of French Railways BB-9004 which, on 29 March 1955, for a distance of $1\frac{1}{4}$ miles near Ychoux on the Bordeaux-Dax main line, attained the incredible speed on rails of $205\frac{3}{5}$ mph with a three-coach train. A speed of 185 mph had been reached after travelling 13 miles; this was maintained for $7\frac{1}{2}$ miles, and for nearly four miles over 199 mph was recorded. These spectacular achievements had to be shared with locomotive CC-7107, which had done precisely the same thing the previous day on the same stretch of line.

The 1,500 volt DC locomotive BB-9004 was built in 1953 by the Société de Materiel de Traction Electrique at a cost of £95,000. Like its rival, it was designed for the haulage of heavy passenger-trains at high speeds. Its continuous rating was 4,000 hp, its wheel diameter 4ft $\frac{1}{8}$in. and with an overall length of 53 ft its weight was only 81 tons. Extremely light on maintenance, one of its best haulage performances was to take a train of 814 tons over the 318 miles between Lyon and Paris at an average speed of $79\frac{1}{2}$ mph.

Photo: Museo Nazionale della Scienza e della Tecnica Leonardo da Vinci, Milan

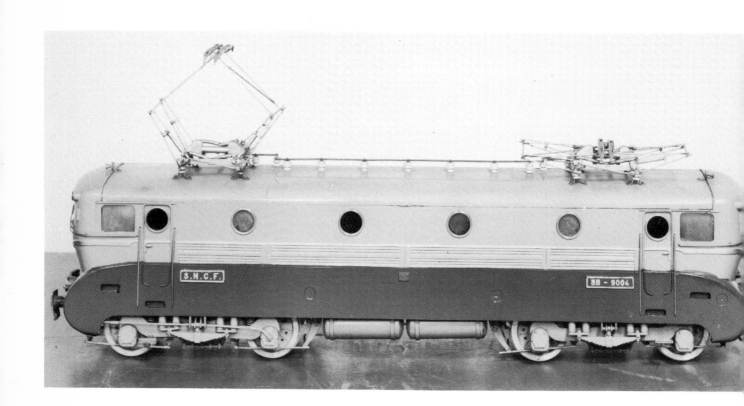

India. Vulcan Foundry and English Electric together built seven 3,600 hp Co-Co electric locomotives for the 5ft 6in. gauge Central system of the Indian Railways in 1954–1955. The Central had been formed four years earlier by an amalgamation of the Great Indian Peninsula, Nizam's State, Scindia State and Dholpur State Railways. The locomotives were similar in design and appearance to those of the Santos-Jundiai and RENFE supplied a few years previously, the principal difference being a line voltage of 1,400 DC instead of 3,000 DC. They were designed for the Bombay–Poona (119 miles) and Bombay–Igatpuri (84 miles) sections.

Overall length and width of these locomotives are 68ft 4¼in. and 10ft 6in. respectively, the weight being 122⅛ tons. They have a maximum tractive effort of 69,000lb. and a top speed of 75 mph, which is attained with 4ft-diameter wheels. Shawcraft Models made the ½in. to 1ft scale publicity model for English Electric. It has all external details and is finished in the correct livery of black with red lining and lettering.
Photo: GEC Traction Ltd

Australia. Models of Western Australian Government Railways locomotives in three scales—10mm., ¼in. and ⅛in.—have been made by H. Clarkson & Son. The example illustrated, of class XA 2-Do-2 diesel electric locomotive No. 1416 *Niligara*, is one of three constructed in ⅛in. scale in 1957. The full-size *Niligara* was part of an order for 48 1,105 hp locomotives fulfilled by Metropolitan-Vickers Electrical Co. in 1954. There were 32 class A and 16 class XA engines, the only difference between them being that the XAs could be operated in multiple. The power-unit is the Crossley HST V-8 two-cycle engine, having eight cylinders 10½in. × 13½in. There are four series-wound traction-motors rated at 650v, 280 amps at 1,408 rpm. Both driving and bogie wheels have a diameter of 2ft 7½in.

With an overall length of 51ft 8in. and width of 8ft 10in. these locomotives weigh 77½ tons, of which 40 tons are adhesive, and are capable of a maximum speed of 55mph. Their starting tractive effort is 27,000 lb and when they were built they were claimed as the most powerful in the world with with an axle-loading limitation of ten tons. Passenger-services worked include Perth to Kalgoorlie, 380 miles, to Albany, 340 miles, and to Meekatharra, 600 miles. Up to 8,000 miles a month are recorded on these runs.
Photo: H. Clarkson & Son

Brazil. The metre-gauge Rede Ferroviaria do Nordeste, formerly the Great Western of Brazil, ordered 13 A1A-A1A 1,000 hp diesel-electric locomotives from the English Electric Co. in 1954, the mechanical parts for which were supplied by the Vulcan Foundry. Two traction-motors were mounted on the outer axles of each bogie. Up to three locomotives could be coupled together and driven in multiple from one cab.

These locomotives went into service between Recife and Afogadas de Ingazeira (250 miles) and between Recife and Maceio (216 miles). They accomplished return trips over either route without refuelling. H. Clarkson & Son made one of these locomotives for the English Electric Co. model in 1954. It is built to ½in. scale and is fully detailed.
Photo: H. Clarkson & Son

Britain. The class 9 2-10-0s were probably the most versatile and the most popular of the standard steam-locomotives constructed by British Railways. Despite their bulk, R. A. Riddles managed to give their design an impressive outline, which this model of No. 92000, the first of the class, recaptures most convincingly. It was made by H. Clarkson & Son in 1955 for the British Transport Commission, the scale being $\frac{1}{2}$in. to 1ft.

No. 92000 went into service at the beginning of 1954. It had two cylinders 20in. × 28in., coupled wheels 5ft and a working-pressure of 250lb./in.^{2}, at 85 per cent of which the tractive effort was 39,667lb. Its boiler, similar in many respects to those of the BR standard Pacifics, had a total evaporative heating-surface of 2,015 sq. ft, supplemented by 535 sq. ft of the superheater. The grate was of the rocking type, area being 40$\frac{1}{5}$ sq. ft. The tender held seven tons of coal and 5,000 gallons of water and the operational weight of locomotive and tender was 139$\frac{1}{5}$ tons.

With their good riding and free-running qualities these grand engines were at home at the head of fast passenger and heavy freight trains alike. Despite their 5ft coupled wheels, speeds attained sometimes reached the eighties. A total of 251 were placed in service, and to No. 92220, completed in 1960, fell the melancholy distinction of being the last steam-locomotive to be built by British Railways.

Photo: H. Clarkson & Son

Britain. Britain's first main-line electrification, providing for electric working of all passenger and freight services, was formally brought into use on 14 September 1954, when Sir Brian Robertson, then Chairman of the British Transport Commission, inaugurated electrically hauled passenger services between Manchester and Sheffield. Approved by the London & North Eastern Railway in 1936, the 1,500 volt DC overhead-line conductor scheme had been seriously delayed by the war. A fleet of 58 Bo+Bo and seven Co-Co electric locomotives was built for the new services. In readiness for the occasion, two ½in. scale-models, one of each type, had been commissioned by the present author, then London Midland public relations & publicity officer. The model of Bo+Bo No. 26020 was made by Bonds O'Euston Road Ltd and that of Co-Co No. 27000 by Cherry's (Surrey) Ltd. Although they were for publicity purposes and were non-working, all external details were embodied and in the driving-cabs the interior equipment was carefully reproduced. The external finish in both cases was the contemporary black with red lining and embellished with yellow Gill Sans numerals and yellow and red lion-on-wheel emblems.

The first Bo+Bo, No. 6701 (later No. 6000 and finally No. 26000) had, in fact, been completed by the LNER in 1941. After satisfactory tests on the Manchester-Altrincham line the locomotive, now No. 6000, was lent in 1947 to the Netherlands Railways, to accomplish 400 miles daily hauling 330 ton passenger-trains at 65 mph or 1,600 ton freight trains at 40 mph. Valuable data was thus obtained before the remainder of the class was built. For both classes the mechanical parts were made in the railway workshops and the electrical equipment by the Metropolitan-Vickers Electrical Co. Leading particulars are

Type	Bo+Bo	Co-Co
Class	EM1	EM2
Length over buffers	50ft 4in.	59ft
Wheel diameter	4ft 2in.	3ft 7in.
Weight in working order	86¾ tons	102½ tons
Maximum tractive effort	45,000lb	45,000lb
Continuous tractive effort	14,600lb	21,100lb
Number of traction motors	Four	Six
Maximum speed	65 mph	90 mph

The first Bo+Bo was withdrawn from service in 1969 after having covered 700,000 miles on British and Dutch metals. Six of the Co-Cos were sold to the Netherlands Railways in the same year, the seventh being cannibalised for spares. *Photos: British Railways*

Sweden. As late as 1955 Sweden was still developing rod-drive for long-distance electric-locomotives when elsewhere individually actuated axles had become almost a general rule. The prototype class Dm 1-D+D-1 locomotive of 6,500 hp was introduced in that year by the Swedish State Railways for working heavy iron-ore trains. Asea were responsible for its electrical equipment and Motala for the mechanical parts. With its 5ft ½in. coupled wheels it was designed to move a maximum of 3,444 tons up 1 in 100 gradients. Its weight is 167 3/10 tons and maximum speed 75 kmph.

In contrast two experimental class Ra 3,600 hp Bo-Bo locomotives Nos. 846 and 847 also appeared in 1955. Carried on 4ft 3in. wheels, they were designed for a maximum speed of 93 kmph. They turned the scale at 62 tons, due to the special efforts made to effect a reduction in weight. As a result, the locomotives achieved the remarkable power/weight ratio of only 37⅕lb./hp, the highest in the world at the time of their construction. Eight more were built, followed by six class Rb and finally 75 class Rc. All are still in service.

The Railway Museum at Gävle displays these 1/10th scale-models of the Dm and Ra locomotives. The former is a

replica of No. 942–943 and was the work of A. B. Sverre of Gothenburg in 1956. The other, of No. 846, was made by Nohab (formerly Nydqvist & Holm) and the Railway Museum in the previous year.
Photos: Railway Museum, Gävle

East Africa. At the time of their construction the 59th class 4-8-2+2-8-4s Nos. 5901–5934 of East African Railways were the most powerful metre-gauge locomotives in the world; at 85 per cent of the boiler pressure their tractive effort was 83,350lb. As built by Beyer Peacock & Co. in 1955 the 7ft 6in. diameter boiler was oil-fired, but the fire-hole was designed to house a mechanical stoker should coal-firing be adopted. The four cylinders were 20½in. × 28in., the coupled wheels 4ft 6in. and the boiler-pressure 225lb./in.² Timken roller-bearing axleboxes were provided throughout. The total

heating-surface, including superheater, was 4,308 sq. ft and the grate-area amounted to 72 sq. ft. The length over buffers of these impressive engines was 104ft 2in. and, with 2,700 gallons of oil-fuel and 8,600 gallons of water, they weighed no less that 252 tons.

The immaculate model of No. 5927 was supplied to Beyer Peacock & Co. by Bassett-Lowke Ltd in 1955. It was made to a scale of ¾in. to 1ft and is complete in every external detail.
Photo: Bassett-Lowke Ltd

Ghana. Diesel-electric locomotives began to replace steam on the 3ft 6in. gauge Gold Coast Government (now Ghana) Railways in 1955. Fourteen 750 hp mixed-traffic Bo-Bo units were supplied that year by English Electric. They were followed later by 23 more of the same type. They measure 35ft in length over buffer-beams, are carried on 36½in. diameter wheels and weigh 53½ tons in operational order. Their maximum service speed is 55 mph and on the heavier main-line duties are worked in multiple. The model of No. 777 illustrated was made in the Apprentice School at Vulcan Foundry. It was completed in 1955 to a scale of ½in. to 1ft, the livery being cream with green bands and lower panels.
Photo: GEC Traction Ltd

Britain. The *Deltic* 3,300 hp Co-Co diesel-electric locomotive, built by the English Electric Co. in 1955, has already passed into history. It occupies a prominent place in the Science Museum at South Kensington, for it was a milestone in diesel-electric traction development in Britain. Although the *Deltic* was the first single-unit diesel-electric locomotive in the world to possess over 3,000 installed horsepower, its real significance was the increased power in relation to weight which it achieved. With a weight of 106 tons its power/weight ratio was equal to 72lb. of locomotive weight for 1 hp. This compared with the 85lb. per hp of the contemporary Krauss-Maffei 2,000 hp diesel-hydraulic locomotive.

Developed by D. Napier & Son Ltd, the lightweight diesel-engine was an 18-cylinder opposed-piston, water-cooled unit, operating in the two-stroke cycle. The cylinders were arranged in three banks of six, each bank containing a crankshaft. In end-view the cylinders formed an equilateral triangle. There were two main generators, each with an output of 1,080 kw, connected to the main output-shaft of the engine. Six traction-motors were provided, three to each bogie, the axleboxes of which were fitted with Timken roller-bearings. The *Deltic* was capable of a top speed of 90 mph and of negotiating a six-chain radius curve.

In revenue-earning service of some 270,000 miles it achieved a reputation for reliable and competent service performance. From its design the British Railways type 55 locomotive was derived. More than one excellent scale-model of the *Deltic* was produced for English Electric for publicity purposes. The example shown was made to a scale of ½in. to 1ft by Edward Exley Ltd and is now in the safe keeping of GEC Traction Ltd. Its external finish repeats the rather flamboyant style of its prototype—light blue body, with yellow lining, grey roof and grey bogies.
Photo: GEC Traction Ltd

Australia. Three ½in. scale-models of New South Wales Government Railways electric-locomotives were made by H. Clarkson & Son in 1954 for Metropolitan-Vickers Electrical Co. Ltd, one of which is illustrated. They preceded the 3,820 hp, 108 ton prototype, 40 of which were constructed by Metropolitan-Vickers, the first reaching Sydney in 1956.

These massive locomotives, the most powerful ever built in Britain at the time, were for use on the main line between Sydney and Lithgow, crossing the Blue Mountains. They were equipped with regenerative braking and for working in multiple, so that 2,000 ton coal-trains as well as passenger-trains could be handled over the steep gradients on the line.
Photo: H. Clarkson & Son

Italy. In 1959 the class E646 Bo-Bo-Bo 3,000 volt DC electric locomotives of the Italian State Railways were introduced for the haulage of fast and heavy trains between Milan, Bologna, Florence and Rome. They are regarded as one of the best designs of recent years. They were developed from the class E428 locomotive of 1935. The latter has a maximum speed of 75 mph and axle-loading of 18¼ tons, compared with 90 mph and 16⅔ tons of the newer design, which is less in weight at 108 tons although more powerful.

The accompanying photograph of a 1/20th scale-model of a class E646 locomotive exemplifies the uncluttered compactness of the design. The lefthand end of the model is cut away to show part of the interior.
Photo: Museo Nazionale della Scienza e della Tecnica Leonardo da Vinci, Milan

U.S.S.R. Many well-finished scale-models of diesel-electric and electric locomotives, complete in all external details, have been made in the Visual Teaching Aids workshops of the USSR Ministry of Communications for instruction and training of railway staff. This is a typical example. It was made in 1961 and reproduces to 1/10th scale No. 0004, one of the Co-Co class TEP diesel-electric express passenger-locomotives. The full-size prototype was completed in 1960. Of 3,000 hp, its length is 63ft and its operational weight 129 tons. The maximum permissible speed is 100 mph, but it is said that on trial 118 mph was attained.
Photo: USSR Railways

Britain. This panorama of railway motive-power development is concluded with a model of a locomotive that is a milestone in the history of the railways of the country where railways began. It is a ½in. to 1ft super-detail scale-replica of Bo-Bo 3,300 hp electric-locomotive No. E3001 of British Railways, for whom it was made in 1962 by H. Clarkson & Son. It depicts the full-size prototype as originally completed in 1960, with two pantographs and finished in the livery style then introduced. This embodied white cab roofs, a blue body and raised chronium letters, numerals and lion-and-wheel crest, the latter from the heraldic achievement of the British Transport Commission.

No. E3001 was the first of the 100 sleek 25Kv ac electric greyhounds now handling all the high-speed main-line traffic between London, Birmingham, Stoke-on-Trent, Manchester and Liverpool. Built in five batches, their electrical equipment was designed by the three contractors concerned—Associated Electrical Industries, English Electric and General Electric—to give a range of variations, so that a comparison of their merits in service could be made. But the cabs were substantially the same and the driving-technique was identical. British Thomson-Houston Co., which became part of AEI Traction Division, made 25 of the locomotives, beginning with No. E3001. The mechanical parts were subcontracted to Birmingham Railway Carriage & Wagon Co. Maximum use was made of glass-fibre construction for components such as cab-roofs, doors, bulkheads, air-ducts and even the transformer oil-conservator tank, in order to achieve light weight. The body was designed so that the locomotive could be completely opened at the top, between cab-bulkheads, for removal of equipment.

The vital statistics of No. E3001 include 4ft diameter wheels, a length over buffers of 56½ft, a total weight of 79⅝ tons, a maximum starting tractive effort of 48,000 lb and a continuous tractive effort of 20,000 lb. Its maximum speed is 100 mph, which is a foretaste of the much higher pace British Railways expresses are likely to attain before another decade has elapsed.
Photo: British Railways

INDEX OF COUNTRIES REPRESENTED

BIBLIOGRAPHY

The British Steam Railway Locomotive from 1825 to 1925, Journal of the Historical Model Railway Society, Journal of Irish Railway Record Society, *Locomotive Magazine*, *Modern Railways*, *Railway Magazine*.

INDEX

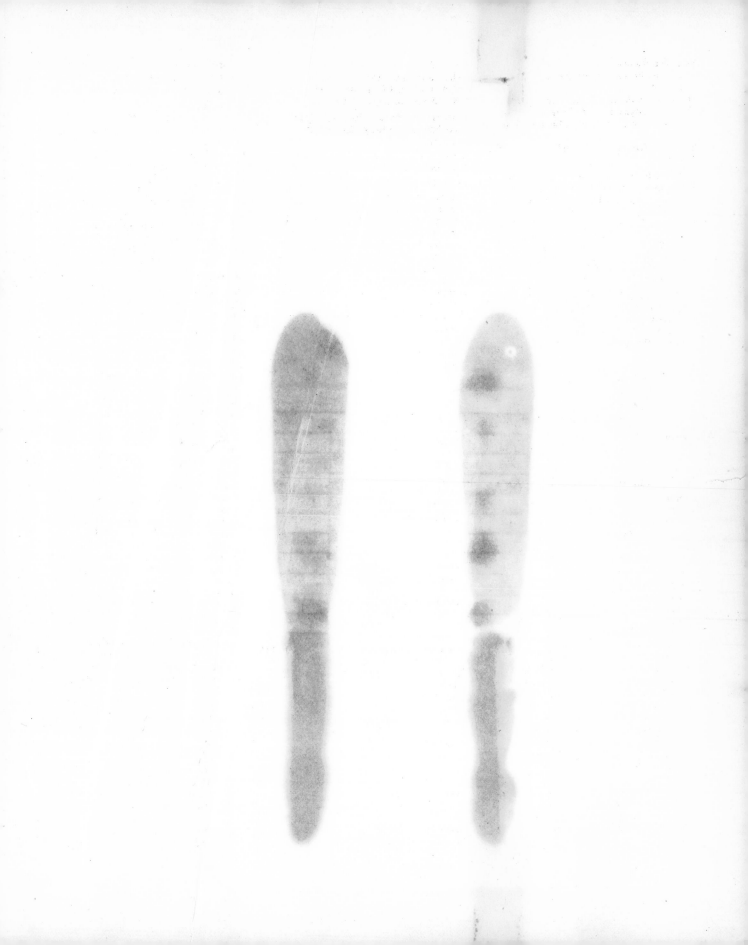